GENDER MATTERS

A manual on addressing gender-based violence affecting young people

Contributors

Dennis van der Veur
Karolina Vrethem
Gavan Titley
Györgyi Tóth

Final editor of activities

Yael Ohana

General editor

Gavan Titley

Coordination and final edition

Goran Buldioski
Annette Schneider

www.coe.int/compass

The views expressed in this manual are the responsibility of the authors and do not necessarily reflect the opinions of the Council of Europe.

Copyright of this publication is held by the Council of Europe. No parts of this publication may be reproduced or transmitted for commercial purposes in any form or by any means, electronic (CD-Rom, Internet, etc.) or mechanical including photocopying, recording or any information storage or retrieval system, without the permission in writing from the Public Information and Publishing Division (publishing@coe.int), Directorate of Communication of the Council of Europe.

Reproduction of material from this publication is authorised for non-commercial education purposes only and on condition that the source is properly quoted.

All correspondence related to this publication or the reproduction or translation of all or part of it should be addressed to:
Council of Europe, Youth Department
European Youth Centre Budapest
1024 Budapest, Zivatar utca 1-3
E-mail: eycb.secretariat@coe.int

Design: Daniel Horvath, http://danielhorvath.com
Proofreading: Rachel Appleby
Published by the Youth Department

ISBN: 978-92-871-6393-6
© Council of Europe, 2007
Reprint, 2013
Printed in Hungary

Table of contents

Preface 7
Acknowledgements 8
Introduction 9

1. Approaching gender

1.1 Why is it so important to consider gender? 15
1.2 What is gender? 17
    1.2.1 Ideas of gender 17
    1.2.2 Gender and sex 19
    1.2.3 Discussing gender 21
1.3 Gender and socialisation 23
    1.3.1 Living in society 23
    1.3.2 Approaches to socialisation 23
    1.3.3 Gendering 26
    1.3.4 Gender and sexuality 27
    1.3.5 Gender and inequality 28
1.4 Masculinities 29
    1.4.1 Case study: The context of young men's lives in Northern Ireland ... 31
1.5 Politics of gender: movements for a more equal society . 34
    1.5.1 Women's movements 34
    1.5.2 Lesbian, Gay, Bisexual and Transgendered Movements . 35
    1.5.3 Mens' groups and Boys' groups 37

2. Gender-based violence

2.1 Introduction 43
2.2 What is violence? 45
    2.2.1 Aggression and violence 46
    2.2.2 Abuse and violent incidents 47
    2.2.3 Violence in the public and private sphere 49

2.3 Types of Violence 51

2.4 Gender-based violence in a human rights framework. 57

2.5 Gender-based violence against LGBT 60

2.6 Domestic violence or violence in intimate relationships 60

    2.6.1 Domestic violence in LGBT relationships. 63

Endnotes for Chapter 2. 66

3. Mobilising against gender inequality and gender-based violence

3.1 Gender in youth work: perspectives and challenges 67

    3.1.1 Gender in youth work practices. 68

3.2 Gender mainstreaming in youth training and youth projects 70

    3.2.1 Gender mainstreaming 71

    3.2.2 Gender mainstreaming and gender equality. 72

    3.2.3 Guidelines and instruments for gender mainstreaming 73

    3.2.4 Gender mainstreaming in training 74

    3.2.5 Ethics and competence in gender training 75

3.3 Taking action against gender-based violence 78

    3.3.1 Identifying whether forms of gender-based violence are present in your youth organisation or group 78

    3.3.2 Youth groups and work in broader coalitions. 79

Endnotes for Chapter 3. 80

4. Exercises addressing gender and gender-based violence with young people

4.1 Working with gender and gender-based violence in the context of (non-formal) education with young people 81

4.2 Human Rights Education – an educational approach 82

    4.2.1 Knowledge, skills, attitudes and values supporting human rights education. . . 83

    4.2.2 Experiential learning – a basis for human rights education 84

    4.2.3 Facilitating human rights education in various settings 85

4.3 Using the Exercises 85
    4.3.1 Choosing exercises 85
    4.3.2 Key to the presentation of the exercises 86
    4.3.3 Advice for the facilitation of the exercises presented in this manual 87

4.4 List of activities 92
    Expectations and demands 93
    Gaining Status 95
    Gender Confusion 97
    Gender-in-a-box 100
    Good, Better, Best 106
    Just Once 110
    Kati's story 114
    Listen Closely 121
    Media Bash 123
    Safety in my life 126
    Sex sells? 130
    Spaces and Places 133
    Stella 136
    The knight on the white horse 139
    Too Hard to Ask 143
    What to do 147
    General exercises for single sex groups 151

5. Appendices - International Legal Human Rights Instruments Related to Gender-Based Violence

The Universal Declaration of Human Rights (Summary) 157

Universal Declaration of Human Rights 158

The European Convention on Human Rights (Simplified Version) 162

Convention on the Elimination of All Forms of Discrimination
    against Women - CEDAW (Summary) 164

Convention on the Elimination of All Forms of Discrimination
    against Women - CEDAW 166

gender matters

Preface

Gender-based violence is one of the most widespread forms of human rights abuse and a violation of human dignity anywhere.

Gender-based violence is a problem in all the member states of the Council of Europe and affects millions of women, men and children regardless of their social status, cultural or religious background, civil status or sexual orientation.

One of the primary aims of the Council of Europe is the safeguard and protection of human rights. Gender-based violence undermines the core values on which the Council of Europe is based and to which its member states have subscribed.

What is special with gender-based violence is that it often happens in private but it does not mean that it should be treated as a private issue. The prevention of gender-based violence and the protection and assistance to the victims is, ultimately, the responsibility of the public authorities while the civil society also has a very important role.

Legal action, however essential, cannot be the only response if we want to reduce and eradicate such forms of violence. The values of human rights, non-violence and gender equality can be neither imposed nor simply advertised; they have to be accepted and respected in real life. The key is education, information and awareness-raising. Only through combined efforts can we secure that the patterns of oppression and humiliation are not repeated from generation to generation.

The Council of Europe has been seriously working on these issues for many years. The Integrated Project "Responses to violence in everyday life" has played an important role in identifying priorities for action and examples of good practice at all levels. The campaign Stop Domestic Violence Against Women launched a year ago is the latest initiative to mobilise all the partners concerned at European and national level.

The role of young people and youth work in this respect is very important. The Youth Programme on Human Rights Education carried out by the Directorate of Youth and Sport works to mainstream human rights education in youth work and to develop a culture of human rights.

This manual - "GENDER MATTERS" - builds on the educational resources and experience of COMPASS, the manual on human rights education with young people. It provides practitioners in human rights education with specific education tools and insights for a gender-sensitive approach to human rights education.

We hope that practitioners and activists in human rights education will find in this manual inspiration and resources to help them in their work.

Maud de Boer-Buquicchio
Deputy Secretary General

Acknowledgments

Thanks are due to many people that have invested themselves in one way or another in order to produce and complete this manual. In particular we would like to acknowledge the following people whose contributions were extremely appreciated:

Rui Gomes and Antje Rothemund for their invaluable and continuous support, comments, dedication and advice.

The trainers and participants on the two training courses on gender-based violence held at the European Youth Centre Budapest in 2004 and 2006 for producing, developing and testing the manual.

The Directorate General of Human Rights, Equality Division for their suggestions of improvement.

Judit Wirth for her comments and additions to the content of the manual.

Finally also, to Merit Ulvik for her tireless work and consistency to the finer details of the manual.

Introduction

Welcome to GENDER MATTERS. This manual is a resource for working on issues of gender and gender-based violence affecting young people, with young people.

Working with young people on issues relating to gender and gender-based violence is a central part of human rights education: educational programmes and activities that focus on promoting equality in human dignity. Over recent years, the Directorate of Youth and Sport of the Council of Europe has worked with youth organisations, associations, initiatives and networks to make human rights education a central aspect of European youth work and citizenship. Developed in relation to other work areas such as intercultural learning, political participation, empowerment of minorities and young people from minority backgrounds, human rights education has the potential to be a catalyst for a range of educational, political and cultural actions. Human rights education is a profound and challenging area for youth workers; it involves rights that are universal, indivisible and inalienable, but also the subject of political marginalisation, interpretation and challenge.

The Directorate of Youth and Sport, particularly through the European Youth Centres in Strasbourg and Budapest and the European Youth Foundation, has acquired a widely recognised expertise for developing and implementing educational approaches, activities and resources that can be adapted to both formal and non-formal educational settings, as well as across different social and cultural realities in Europe. Ongoing events in Europe and the wider world give this work a constant urgency, as moves towards a 'culture of peace' are challenged by new conflicts and risks.

In this context, a Human Rights Education Youth Programme was launched in 2000 with the aim to bring human rights education into the mainstream of youth policy and youth work practice. Since the beginning of this programme, the Directorate of Youth and Sport held numerous activities to address the issues surrounding gender and violence and involving young people in the prevention of gender-based violence. An integrated project 'Responses to violence in everyday life in democratic society', was instigated by the Council of Europe in 2002.

The expression of need for educational material dealing specifically with these issues of gender-based violence was born in the recommendations from the "Violence Against Young Women in Europe" seminar that took place at the European Youth Centre, Budapest in 2001. The outcome of this and numerous other seminars produced recommendations which are summarised in the publication "Young People and Violence Prevention – Youth Policy Recommendations". This publication built the basis of the work of the 7th European Conference of Ministers Responsible for Youth that took place in Budapest, 2005. The subject of gender-based violence got special attention in the final recommendation of this conference in paragraph 5:

gender matters

In order to prevent gender-related violence, notably against children and young people, homophobic violence and the sexual exploitation of children and young people, governments should include a priority focus on gender equality, sexuality and power in their youth policy agendas.

Addressing gender-based violence is particularly relevant in the work priorities of the Directorate of Youth and Sport, especially those dealing with human rights education and social cohesion. This is emphasized by the following projects and objectives:

- developing networks of trainers and multipliers in human rights education with young people;
- supporting and promoting good practice in human rights education and intercultural dialogue at local level;
- supporting the recognition of human rights education and intercultural dialogue in formal and non-formal education;
- empowering young people to be actors in preventing all forms of violence;
- developing the capacity of youth organisations and multipliers to address all forms of violence.

> For more information or to get involved in the "Stop Domestic Violence Against Women" campaign, visit the website http://www.coe.int/t/dg2/equality/domesticviolencecampaign

The Council of Europe broader activities also continue to work towards raising the awareness of European citizens on gender-based violence and putting an end to it through campaigns such as the "Stop Domestic Violence Against Women" campaign and the work of the Equality between Women and Men division[1].

The COMPASS points in new directions: gender and gender-based violence

> You can find COMPASS online at www.coe.int/compass

Within the framework of the Council of Europe's Human Rights Education Youth Programme – "COMPASS - a manual on Human Rights Education with Young People" was produced and launched in 2002 in order to make human rights education accessible, usable and useful to educators, facilitators, leaders, teachers, volunteers and trainers who are active in educational activities with young people. It does this by providing a wide range of approaches, themes and methods together with 49 practical activities to engage, involve and motivate young people to form a positive awareness of human rights in their own ways and in their own communities.

In a sense, human rights education addresses all aspects of life today, and one of the most important aspects of COMPASS is the overview it provides of key issues and areas of life where human rights are often violated and under threat. This overview points to central issues that human rights education can and should address, and also to the ways in which issues in human rights education interact. For example, we cannot consider the section on *children and the rights of the child* (pp 317 - 321), without also considering *poverty* (pp 382-86) and *education* (pp 345-50). Human rights education is challenging for precisely this reason: it asks us to combine an overview with some more specific areas of knowledge and experience.

---

1 www.coe.int/T/e/human_rights/equality

This manual is also a response to this challenge; gender equality and inequality has registered in COMPASS (pp 354-358), but this manual is addressed to those who want to take a longer journey in that direction. COMPASS examines the ways in which gender inequalities may take a different shape in different societies, but makes it clear that gender power affects everybody on the planet, in both our private and public lives and worlds.

The aim of GENDER MATTERS is to provide information, perspectives and resources for deepening and widening this focus on gender and human rights.

Why do we need a resource addressing gender and gender-based violence?

At one level, the reason for working on gender and gender issues should be self-evident. Everybody is gendered; we all live to a large extent through an identity as 'man' or 'woman', reflecting on roles we play socially that involve expectations of masculinity and femininity, and living a sexuality that shapes our relations to others while being judged according to prevailing ideas in our societies. Our gendered identities are not static, but change and shift according to our experiences, the contexts we live in, the power we have and the desires we feel. The freedom we have to control and fashion this aspect of our identity depends very much on the absence or presence of different expectations, pressures and prejudices. Gender is something that is with us from the moment we are dressed as a boy or girl at birth, to the types of speeches friends will make at our funerals.

Nevertheless, the writers of GENDER MATTERS have the impression that gender is not a central consideration in many aspects of formal and non formal education and has long been neglected in European youth work and youth policy. While it has become common – in intercultural learning, for example - to reflect on our cultural conditioning and what it means for interaction with others, this very basic reflex has not been accompanied by a similarly basic reflection on gender. There may be many reasons for this:

- Gender is often associated with women's issues and feminism, and therefore seen to have been 'sorted out' or 'yesterday's issue';
- Gender is a very difficult subject to address (personally and educationally) as it asks us to consider intimate aspects of our sense of self, sexuality and behaviour;
- Considering gender means questioning forms of power and privilege that benefit many people, mainly men, in our societies.

Yet when young people are brought together in an educational activity, questions of gender identity, sexuality and power are present (as they are wherever human beings gather in groups of two or more!). GENDER MATTERS aims to remind us of this and to suggest that all youth activities involve thinking about the kinds of environment we provide for young people.

This is especially important when it comes to the presence of gender-based violence in the lives of young people. As chapter two of this manual discusses, various forms of gender-based violence – from violence in the 'private' world of the home to the structural violence of neo-liberal economics – affect the security, dignity and potential of countless young people. The reality of young people throughout Europe and the rest of the world include domestic violence, rape and incest, human trafficking, violence in armed conflict, racism and discrimination, female genital mutilation and other forms of bodily mutilation, economic injustice and social exclusion. Gender-based violence, in all its forms, is a violation of human rights. Young women are particularly vulnerable to the types of violence outlined, as are young people whose sexual identities are marginalised and discriminated against socially and politically. However this manual also pays significant attention to the ways in which *masculinity* – different cultural constructions of 'being a man' – may demand attitudes to violence that inhibit and affect many young men. These young people are not abstract statistics but are present in our schools, youth clubs, organisations, work camps and projects.

If gender is central to human relationships, it is likely that gender-based violence is ever-present in private relationships and our societies in general. While statistics on how often it occurs vary from state to state - and there are significant differences in levels of awareness, political commitment and social provision in different European contexts - *the forms of gender-based violence discussed here exist everywhere*. That is the starting point for this manual, and that is why working on gender awareness and addressing gender-based violence needs to be an integrated aspect of human rights education in Europe. Gender-based violence is not an optional extra in human rights education; it is always already present in the life experiences young people bring with them into educational and youth work contexts. Gender-based violence is a form of human rights abuse that many young people are exposed to, and it is an experience of violence that prevents them from developing and fully exercising their rights.

Using this resource

GENDER MATTERS aims to be a useful introduction to gender and gender-based violence for people who work with young people, by providing:
- A reflection on gender and gender-based violence
- Background legal, political and social information
- Methods and resources for education and training activities with young people.

As a result, it is organised in the following way:

Chapter 1: Approaching Gender gives an overview of different understandings and theories of gender. The emphasis is on gender as a *process*, and on understanding how expectations of gender roles and behaviours are significant for power and possibility in our societies.

Chapter 2: Gender-based violence discusses why gender-based violence has become an important aspect of human rights work; it gives an overview of different kinds of gender-based violence, and the impacts they have on people who have been victimised.

Chapter 3: Mobilising against gender inequality and gender-based violence provides ideas to consider when mobilising against gender-based violence. This is relevant to activism within organisations or associations, and also in the wider campaigning or training work on young activists.

Chapter 4: Exercises addressing gender and gender-based violence with young people comprises exercises for training and facilitation that cover different gender issues and aspects of gender-based violence.

Appendices provide essential information regarding the current European and international human rights instruments related to gender-based violence, including international organisations and institutions that work on issues relating to this.

Although all the exercises have been put in Chapter 4 of the manual which may appear the most 'hands on' resource when addressing gender-based violence with young people, throughout the first three chapters you will also find:

Reflection Boxes – These are guided questions that can be adapted from individual questions for reflection to group orientated questions and facilitated discussions.

Case Boxes – These are real life stories or situations that young people face and have been recorded here. They can be used as examples when illustrating the reality of gender-based violence and its impact on people.

Definition Boxes – These are definitions of uncommon terms that explain them further and can be used for your own knowledge or to explain concepts to others.

Good Practice Boxes – These examples show what some organisations are doing to prevent and fight against gender-based violence and can give you and other people ideas on similar activities that can be organised.

When reading this resource and thinking about its use in your youth work, it is important to consider the question of responsibility:

- Educators have a responsibility to those they work with. This manual is based on the principle that while gender is of relevance to everyone, it does not follow that running safe and ethical explorations of gender in youth work is straightforward. Specific training reflections, approaches and methodologies are necessary. If some exercises are not used carefully and sensitively, they can have an opposite effect on young people and be used to promote stereotypes and work against the prevention of gender-based violence.
- Working with gender – as with other areas of human rights education – is a *competence area*. It always begins with the youth activists working with themselves, and reflecting on the attitudes, beliefs, knowledge and behaviour that a person brings to youth work in general, and work on gender in particular.
- Users don't have to read this manual in its entirety to be able to use it. How much you read (and reflect on) before using the exercises is guided by how competent you feel about the subject, your own skills, your own self-reflection and the needs of your group.

- Topics relating to gender and gender-based violence are sensitive. This sensitivity is not only felt by young people but also by communities, organisations, institutions and governments. To work further in this area together with others, it is necessary to be "tolerant" to the different approaches taken while being firm on the purpose.
- When working with a group of young people, we can never fully know the backgrounds and experiences of the people we work with. The subjects that are raised when discussing gender and gender-based violence can initiate sensitive feelings and uncomfortable discussions for some. It is important to be aware of how the people you work with are reacting and to know how to deal with situations before they arise. For more advice on how to do this, read further the introduction to the exercises in Chapter 4.

A final point needs to be made about the translation of this resource into different societies and contexts. The authors of GENDER MATTERS have tried to use sources and examples from a range of places in the Europe of the Council of Europe and beyond. Inevitably, however, we are guided by what we know, and more importantly, by what we do not know! This manual asks those who read it to be interpreters, not necessarily translating from one language to another, but from one context to another. The reader will need to supplement the information provided here with information from, for example, their own national realities, institutions and NGOs. In addition, we hope that readers will take the time and make the effort to reflect and decide where different perspectives do not fit their experience and youth work context, and adapt and substitute examples, ideas and explanations.

1. Approaching gender

1.1 Why is it so important to consider gender?

Does your gender determine your sexuality? Do you have to explain your gender to other people? How often do you think about your gender?

Gender is everywhere and nowhere. If we look at some international news stories when we were writing this in the first months of 2005, it seems as if gender is everywhere: a Mexican woman was denied the chance to play professional football for a men's second division club because FIFA (the game's world governing body) insists on 'gender-specific competitions'; in the same week, the international development organisation Action Aid[2] launched a report that demonstrates that violence is preventing girls from attending school in many countries in the world, and noted that "violence that effects girls in or around schools is but one aspect of violence against girls in general"; during the US Presidential election in the United States the Vice-President Dick Cheney constantly mocked the Democratic Party candidate John Kerry for using the word 'sensitive': real leaders don't talk like that; in the music world, organisations campaigning for the rights of Lesbian, Gay, Bisexual and Transgender people have instigated a global protest against 'murder music'; specifically dancehall reggae from Jamaica where major stars sing songs calling for gay men and lesbian women to be burned and murdered. These are just one reader's impressions. What do you read about in your newspapers? What do you see when you turn on the TV?

However, we could also read these stories and find that gender is nowhere, especially from the perspective of some of the people featured in the stories. Isn't it better that men and women don't compete, especially since men are more *naturally* competitive? Don't leaders have to be strong in certain ways, as a man or especially as a woman? Shouldn't free speech permit people to say what they think is *normal*?

Gender is everywhere because when people interact socially, the way we view ourselves, our identities and our freedoms, our rights and possibilities all come into direct contact with how others see us and how they act in relation to us. At the same time it could be argued that gender is nowhere because the ways in which we see each other socially tend to be so naturalised that they appear to be normal and natural. This manual begins by arguing that engaging with gender is important because to understand how we live together socially means questioning the things we take for granted in our everyday lives.

As the introduction explains, GENDER MATTERS is a resource for working with others, but it is also a resource that underlines the need for constantly working with oneself. In fact, we would argue that one is not possible without the other. In some ways the reasoning behind this can be expressed very easily: each of us is a person with their own subjectiv-

---

2 www.actionaid.org

ity and experiences of living with others in society, and therefore everybody is personally involved in discussions of gender. It is easy to test this out: have you ever seen somebody walking on the street and wondered, because of their appearance, if they are a woman or a man? Have you subsequently asked yourself, 'why do I automatically put them in one category or the other?' Every day, it is possible that we organise the ways we see ourselves and others according to gendered assumptions that we may not think much about. That is why this chapter explores the concept of gender and how it relates to people's subjective sense of themselves, their social experiences and interactions, privileges and obstacles, freedoms and oppressions. Chapter 2 takes the same approach to violence: the world is not divided into violent and non-violent people, even if some people act with far more violence and far more frequently than others. Nobody is free of violence, and youth workers and youth leaders have a special responsibility to think about their attitudes to gender and violence.

You may have heard – in some formulation – of the idea of 'gender awareness'. As with all of the concepts that we will encounter here, there are many different ways of discussing this. However a basic explanation is that we all need to be aware of, and work on our awareness

- that we are likely to perceive and interpret ourselves in the categories of a woman and / or a man, and that these categories do not do justice to how complex our gender and sexual identities are;
- of how we consciously and unconsciously express our gendered selves and express this in relation to others;
- of how we interpret and evaluate the gender of others and how this affects the ways that we interact with them;
- of the images, associations, assumptions and normative standards that we use to interpret the gender(s) and sexualities of others, and where these influences come from;
- of how gender is a key factor in the power, privilege and possibilities that some people have and some people do not have in our societies, and how this affects progress towards equality in our societies.

This section argues that gender awareness is a *necessary* and *ongoing* process for everybody, and particularly for youth workers and young people who want to work on issues of gender and violence with their peers. It is necessary because nobody can completely 'step outside' of the social and cultural processes that impact on our identities, values and perceptions, but that we can develop ways of reflecting and questioning ourselves that are very important for group work and interaction. It is ongoing because gender is a process, and our ways of thinking of ourselves and others as gendered, sexual beings shift over time and in different contexts.

> **Reflection**
>
> Think about your current work in a youth context. Why is gender awareness necessary..
> (a) for yourself? (b) for the young people you are engaging with? (c) for your organisation? (d) for the social context you work in?

1.2 What is gender?

Yes, what is gender? What is the relationship of gender to sex? What does it mean to understand gender as an ongoing process? What does gender have to do with power?

These are basic questions, but they are not easy to answer because gender is an idea that has been discussed and analysed from very different perspectives for many years. Gender is both an *analytical category* – a way of thinking about how identities are constructed – and a *political idea* that addresses the distribution of power in society. Because of this, gender is an area of focus that cuts across thinking about society, law, politics and culture, and is frequently discussed in relation to other aspects of identity and social position, such as class, ethnicity, age and physical abilities. It is also important in a range of social and political debates that are conducted differently according to the cultural context. This section does not intend to define gender because understandings of gender differ and are often disputed. More modestly, its intention is to put forward some ideas that will recur throughout the different sections and chapters, and to invite the reader to consider these in his or her own context.

1.2.1 Ideas of gender

What does it mean to be a woman? What does it mean to be a man? Are we born knowing our gender? What influences our concept of our own gender?

Despite these considerations we can start to build on some straightforward descriptions. Gender can be seen as the ways in which we understand and live as male and female. From birth, our social and cultural contexts offer us meanings, limits and possibilities of being 'woman' or 'man'. The World Health Organisation (WHO) offers a useful summary of this:

> *'Sex' refers to the biological and physiological characteristics that define men and women.*
> *'Gender' refers to the socially constructed roles, behaviours, activities and attributes that society considers appropriate for men and women.*
> *To put it another way: 'male' and 'female' are sex categories, while 'masculine' and 'feminine' are gender categories.* [1]

> **Reflection**
>
> Is this definition different in your language? Do the words 'gender' and 'sex' exist? Is it possible to translate this? How do categories of masculine and feminine work in your language?

gender matters

We learn to identify ourselves in particular ways, and in relation to wider images, codes and assumptions about gender. Importantly, these understandings of gender have an influential bearing on how people are viewed in our societies, and what kinds of possibilities are available or unavailable to them. To accept the idea of gender and the kinds of thinking that follow from it is to accept that being a woman or a man is not only a biological category of being with a fixed, shared meaning, but rather that these are categories that - socially and culturally - we *give meaning* to. Kalyani Menon-Sen expresses this very nicely:

> The term 'gender' is used to describe a set of qualities and behaviours expected from men and women by their societies.
>
> Gender is not biological; girls and boys are not born knowing how they should look, dress, speak, behave, think or react. [2]

If we take this line of thinking further, ideas of gender are likely to differ from context to context over time, and to be understood in relation to other aspects and markers of identity, such as age, class, ethnicity, bodily abilities and sexual orientation.

Analysing gender involves looking at the different ways in which socio-cultural codes of being a woman and man are understood and lived, normalised and regulated, negotiated and challenged. It involves examining *femininities* and *masculinities* as sets of ideas, definitions and practices that people inherit and use to make sense of their identities, appearances and behaviours, and in particular to make sense of their bodies' 'sexual and reproductive capacities' [3]. Analysing gender examines the ways in which apparently obvious and natural differences between women and men have been constructed socially over time, and further examines the ways in which those supposed differences have been central to relationships of power and inequality.

Reflection

According to the quote above, 'gender' refers to the *socially constructed* roles, behaviours, activities and attributes that society considers *appropriate* for men and women.

What do you understand by this idea of socially constructed roles? When do you become aware of it, and when not? Track your understandings of this for a day, for example, when watching television, when do you become conscious of gender roles, and why?

	What?	Who?	(In)Appropriate?	Why?
Role				
Behaviour				
Activity				
Attribute				

1.2.2 Gender and sex

Can people have a different gender to their biological sex? Are there only two types of gender? What is the relationship between our body and our gender – if there is one?

The definitions discussed in the previous section offer a clear differentiation between the idea of sex as a biological category, and gender as the socially constructed ways in which masculinities and femininities are expressed and organised. Feminist thinking, in particular since the 1970s, has distinguished between gender and sex, and the ways in which differences between male and female have been culturally loaded with natural and *essential* meanings. Challenging these naturalised meanings has been central to challenging the idea that men and women should play distinct roles in relation to each other, and that 'all women' or 'all men' should conform to a set of 'natural' expectations.

For many analysts, sex is a biological fact: two biologically differentiated types of children can be born - a girl or a boy. Gender can be understood as everything that shapes understandings and practices of 'being a girl' and 'being a boy' from that moment on. The WHO definitions quoted in the previous section provide the following illustration of this:

> *Aspects of sex will not vary substantially between different human societies, while aspects of gender may vary greatly.*

> *Some examples of sex characteristics:*
- Women can menstruate while men cannot.
- Men have testicles while women do not.
- Women have developed breasts that are usually capable of lactating (producing milk) while men have not.
- Men generally have bigger bones than women.

> *Some examples of gender characteristics:*
- In most countries women earn significantly less than men.
- In Vietnam many more men than women smoke because female smoking has not traditionally been considered appropriate.
- In Saudi Arabia men are allowed to drive cars while women are not.
- In most of the world, women do more housework than men.

> **Reflection**
>
> On what issues and in what ways do you experience sex and gender being confused? Why do you think this is?
> The list of examples provided by WHO has a global scope. Could you add some examples for your own country, or from Europe?

Before we continue to examine the relationship between sex and gender, we should also recognise that it is not as simplistic as it appears. Not all individuals are clearly classifiable as either 'male' or 'female' even on the strictly biological basis denoted here. 'Intersexed' individuals may not be classifiable, as the Eastern Michigan University Lesbian, Gay, Bisexual, Transgender Resource Centre describes:

> *Intersex people are born with 'sex chromosomes', external genitalia or internal reproductive systems that are not considered 'standard' for either male or female. The existence of intersexuals shows that there are not just two sexes and that our ways of thinking about sex (trying to force everybody to fit into either the male box or the female box) is socially constructed.* (4)

Despite the existence of intersex individuals, there is never any question of not making a choice, and of organising gender identities into male and female. Therefore many people argue that sex itself is also a gendered idea that assumes that male bodies will always 'become' men, and that women's identities are limited to those that inhabit a female body.

Nevertheless, many discussions of gender proceed on the basis of a biological division into 'female' and 'male', which over time become gendered identities. For example, in most western countries, if you went to a hospital to visit a newborn girl or boy, and stopped to buy a card, there is a good chance that the congratulations cards for boys and girls are colour coded in a gendered way, that the little girls and boys on the cards are dressed differently, and that they are represented with different kinds of toys. In a wide range of ways – including how the child is dressed, played with, spoken about and to, what they are encouraged and not encouraged to take an interest in – this biologically female or male being is interpreted as and comes to understand themself as a boy or girl. We all learn to operate within assumptions of how girls and boys 'should' be and what they 'normally' do.

As John Hartley has pointed out, "Whenever sexual differences are taken as meaningful, we are in the presence not of sex but of gender… gender is a human and a signifying division, its 'source' in nature is neither here nor there" (5). The idea of gender, therefore, stands in opposition to ideas of 'biological determinism' – the idea that sex has a decisive role in shaping the person and their behaviour – and 'essentialism': a range of ideas that contend that *there just are* different essences of woman and man.

The example of babies receiving blue or pink gifts may be an obvious example, but it is the obvious nature of gender that underlines its power. While gender roles and gender-based assumptions have been diversified and widely challenged, it is important to recognise that gender seems natural because many aspects of it are normalised and reinforced in everyday life. In other words, even if gender is the cultural construction of male and female identities around (mainly) biologically different bodies, these gendered identities become *naturalised.* Some ways of behaving become accepted and privileged over others. Nature, as Hartley observes, may not determine what it means to live as female or male, but assumptions about gender and gender difference are often based on a sense of *what is natural.*

In particular times and places, therefore, gender often involves assumptions that have become normal about what is recognised as being a woman or man. As we shall see, these assumptions are reinforced by patterns of relationships, in social institutions, and in images and information absorbed on a daily basis. Think, for example, of equivalent phrases to these in your language: "He can't help it, he's a man", "boys will be boys", "She's all woman", or generalising phrases such as "women always…", "all men should…" Some contexts, for example, may include a phrase such as "Be a man about it". If we follow through this analysis of gender, this suggests that both the speaker and the listener have an idea, in their context, of what is usually associated with correct male behaviour, and what is not. There is a wide range of assumptions behind phrases such as 'be a man' and 'she is all woman' that the speaker assumes do not need to be spelt out. The phrase is also an order: it suggests that the listener has little control over how their reactions and behaviour will be interpreted if he wants to be interpreted as 'a man' or as 'a woman'.

In the following extract our arguments are very close to the idea that

> […] *qualities that are stereotypically attributed to women and men in contemporary western culture (such as greater emotional expression in women, greater tendencies to violence and aggression in men) are seen as gender, which entails that they could be changed.* (6)

However when we start to analyse gender, and to think about how we invite people to evaluate their behaviour in relation to these reflections, we initially need to recognise that gendered ways of interpreting ourselves and others are very powerful. They are deeply socialised and often appear to be *normal* and *natural*, 'the way things are and have always been', and simply *common sense*. This does not mean that people are entirely trapped by strict gender roles, or that individual agency is powerless in the face of social influences. What it does mean is that dominant, normalised codes of masculinity and femininity are established in everyday practice in most societies, and that people need to recognise how their power stems from the ways in which they become natural and unremarkable.

1.2.3 Discussing gender

Before moving on to examining gender and socialisation, it is important to make some remarks about approaching gender and gender issues in your own context and how this relates to working with young people.

- *Gender is a sensitive issue*: Understandings and feelings about gender and gender issues can often be deeply personal, and approaching these issues can trigger memories and feelings about past or current experiences. When we deal with issues of identity, it is not always possible to know 'who is in the room'. Before engaging in discussions such as these with your youth group, you need to think carefully

> Exercise
>
> Following these sections, it is useful to consider the exercise Gender Boxes.

about how to conduct them sensitively and responsibly. See 3.2.5 for discussions of safety and ethics in training.

- *Gender is a political issue:* Gender and discussions of gender are also often very 'hot' and political, and may bring into question different types of ideological, religious and other firmly held beliefs. Facilitating such discussions or related training courses is challenging and involves being acutely aware of our own attitudes and beliefs and knowing what is necessary to allow others to discuss these issues in a meaningful way.

- *Gender is a language issue*: Despite the definitions and differentiations offered above, you may encounter the terms 'gender' and 'sex' used interchangeably in society. For example, some questionnaires or forms may ask for your 'gender' and simply provide the categories 'male' and 'female' for you to choose from. In many languages, there is not an equivalent division between sex and gender, or gender may have been newly introduced; this is an important point when it comes to national and international youth contexts. This constant shift from one term to another may be an indicator of some of the confusions involved in discussing gender in our societies.

- *Gender is everybody's issue:* Because widespread awareness of gender is primarily a result of feminist politics (which moved from challenging the position and roles of women in society to addressing the formation of gendered subjects) there is also often a tendency to associate gender with women and women's issues alone. The absence of an analysis of men and understandings of men in this assumption tells its own story. Gender involves examining how biologically differentiated bodies accrue meanings as woman or man over time, and *in relation to each other.* It also involves looking at the complex ways in which masculinities and femininities may reinforce each other or also overlap.

- *Gender is a power issue:* Committed gender analysis does not examine the production of male and female identities in relation to each other without considering how these relations are produced in and reproduce *differences in power and equality*. In general these micro and macro relationships tend to privilege men and subordinate women. The sections that follow develop some of the ways in which gendered roles and behaviours propagate inequalities between women and men. Furthermore, it is also important to recognise that "…current norms of gender marginalise many men and that cultural constructions of gender exclude and alienate those who do not fit neatly into the categories of male or female". [7]

1.3 Gender and socialisation

How is gender 'learnt'? Why is gender 'in process'? What influences our values, perceptions and expectations of gender?

1.3.1 Living in society

> *Society is mysterious to us because we have lived in it and it now dwells inside us at a level that is not ordinarily visible from the perspective of everyday life.* (8)

This quotation suggests that we simultaneously experience and learn about society, while not necessarily being aware of how we learn and what we experience. In other words, we may be highly attuned to signs of gender in the environment around us, while not necessarily reflecting on how these signs have become *gendered* for us. The sociologists Zygmunt Bauman and Tim May argue that, "…many of our choices are habitual and so not subject to deliberate and open choice" (9). As they explain, in considering how we learn to live socially with others, how we see ourselves and act is informed to a significant extent by the contexts we live in and the groups and networks we inhabit. In social life we gather an enormous amount of "…tacit knowledge (that) orients our conduct without us necessarily being able to express how and why it operates in particular ways".(10) This everyday knowledge includes a sense of values, norms, roles and ways of evaluating behaviour. For example, without ever consciously learning guidelines about how close we can be to others in public places, we somehow know that there are shared 'rules' about sitting beside others on a metro and not reading the paper over their shoulder.

This kind of knowledge is constantly expanding and being fine-tuned: "although deeply immersed in our daily routines, informed by practical knowledge oriented to the social settings in which we interact, we often do not pause to think about the meaning of what we have gone through; even less frequently do we pause to compare our private experiences with the fate of others…".(11) Thinking about how we *learn* about gender involves a challenge: it invites us to take a critical distance from ourselves and our daily modes of seeing and interacting, and to pause and think about the meaning of gender, and how we might be able to acquire such a vast, common sense, seemingly *natural* knowledge of gender roles, values and identities.

1.3.2 Approaches to socialisation

As humans we are born into socio-cultural arrangements and meanings that pre-date us. 'Socialisation' is the term that is often given to how we learn, from early childhood, to fit into and negotiate the normative expectations for us to be able to behave, in particular in relation to sets of masculine and feminine codes, roles and behaviours. Being born 'he' or 'she' does not merely denote a biological sex category, but marks 'him' and 'her' out as the inheritors of characteristics that women and men should have, preconceptions about how they should behave, play, be played with, dress, react and express emotions. As Jane Pilcher and Imelda Whelehan explain:

> *The concept of socialisation features in explanations of gender difference, where emphasis is given to the process of how individuals learn to become masculine or feminine in their identities, appearance, values and behaviour. The primary stage of socialisation occurs during infancy and childhood, via interaction between adults (especially parents) and children. Socialisation is, though, a life-long process. As individuals grow up and older, they continually encounter new situations and experiences and so learn new aspects of femininity and masculinity throughout their lives.* (12)

However, knowing that something called socialisation takes place is different from analysing how socialisation takes place, and this is a particularly challenging discussion given the very many contexts in which a resource such as this one may be read. A key concern for anthropologists who study gender, for example, is that the ways in which women and men relate to each other and interact, and the social senses in which the sexes themselves are conceptualised vary enormously from place to place. With this in mind, we can talk about socialisation in two ways. It is (a) a general idea of processes that to a certain extent shape and orient us over time through our interaction with others, resulting in the acquisition of a gendered identity, and (b) a concept that has a more specific history in sociology.

Generally, ideas of socialisation suggest that we learn about prevalent gender roles, differences and values through interaction with important agents. These include the family, teachers in our educational experience, peer groups and our reception of mediated images and information. This general idea becomes more complicated when we look at the divergence of views that surround how socialisation takes place. Key questions include:

- How much importance should different agents of socialisation be given in our considerations?
- To what extent and in what ways are people able to actively negotiate these influences and to fashion a gender identity more consciously?

Theories of role-learning, which were most influential in the 1970s and which have become a form of common sense, argue that children learn and internalise *correct* gender roles and behaviours through interaction with adults, especially their parents. In everyday situations, it is argued, parents often sanction and set boundaries of *appropriate* gendered behaviour for children, such as what games and toys to play with, and also implicitly offer themselves as gendered role models through their own behaviour. Children learn to travel as girls or boys by using maps that reflect the important directions laid down by key adult influencers. Thus, across theories of socialisation that emphasise role-acquisition, recurring ideas include the ways in which boundaries for behaviour – the rigidity of which depend on the context – are reinforced by logics of positive and negative reaction, resulting in norms for feminine and masculine roles and behaviours being *internalised*.

Agency (personal involvement) *in gender construction:* although we are not able to do full justice to the finer points of role-learning theories here, it is nevertheless valid to point out limits to this kind of approach. This kind of approach may be useful for suggesting how 'dominant' or 'hegemonic' gender roles are formed, but it cannot account for the development of women and men that oppose sexism and heterosexism (sexism directed at people on the basis of sexual orientation). Neither does it explain how in many ways gender roles have become more complex and confused. Why do some people seem to accept and live within certain roles, and others reject or subvert them?

For example, a stereotypical gender role constructs a man as a father working outside the home, and associates the male historically with the role of soldier, at the same time, in a few European countries it is becoming increasingly common to see fathers who have both been in the army for national service and taken parental leave to be the primary carer of a child. Similarly, while schools have been identified as associated with stereotyped femininities and masculinities, in many contexts this assertion does not stand up to analysis, given the changes in the ways in which educational materials and curricula now reflect an increased sensitivity to gender.

Perhaps most importantly, over-emphasising socialisation as a force that guarantees conformity is as limiting as denying the influence of society on the *individual*. After all, the educational logic of this resource is based on a belief that our understandings of gender can change, and that people can and do adapt gender norms in their own lives. Therefore, many contemporary theories of gender emphasise the power that people have to *reflect on, shape and construct their own gender identities*. Young people in particular, in their use of style, popular culture and their own networks have, in many contexts, increased autonomy when it comes to how they represent themselves and live in their bodies.

Therefore, many accounts tend to opt for a balance between accounts of socialisation and the autonomy of the individual:

> *We adopt different masculinity and femininity practices depending on our situations and beliefs. Our understandings of gender are dynamic, changing over time with maturity, experience and reflection. Thus we are active in constructing our own gender identities, but the options available to us are not unlimited. We are influenced by the collective practices of institutions such as school, church, media and family, which construct and reinforce particular forms of masculinity and femininity.* [13]

Alsop, Fitzsimons and Lennon mention the following three ways in which aspects of gender socialisation interact:
- *Gender as a feature of subjectivity*: "We identify and make sense of ourselves as men and women or boys and girls". This will depend on the people, institutions and contexts in which we live, and the social expectations to perform and be recognised as gendered in particular ways that we encounter.

- Therefore we can talk about *Gender as the cultural understandings and representations we encounter*. "The belief that girls like sitting and playing with dolls, whereas boys like rough-and-tumble play has traditionally formed part of some cultures' understanding of gender difference in childhood".
- Such understandings inform *Gender as a social variable*. Gender "structures the pathways of those so classified within society. In the field of work, for instance, there is still a tendency for men and women to be channelled into doing different jobs and by consequence to earn different rates of pay". (14)

1.3.3 Gendering

If, as we have discussed, gender is a dynamic process, then gender can also be discussed as a verb: to gender. As Pilcher and Whelehan explain,

> *The shift to using gender as a verb (to gender, gendered, gendering, engendered) is a reflection of changed understandings of gender as an active ongoing process, rather than as something that is ready-made and fixed. In this sense, then, something is gendered when it is, in and of itself, actively engaged in social processes that produce and reproduce distinctions between men and women.* (15)

With this quotation in mind, read the extract below and reflect on how it presents gendering as a dynamic process. It is taken from the novel *Populärmusik från Vittula* (translated into English as *Popular Music*). The author, Mikael Niemi, describes what it was like for a group of boys to grow up in a small town in northern Sweden on the border with Finland in the 1960s. This short extract discusses how the boys, who have started a rock band, examine whether or not playing this new music is 'knapsu':

> *In the early days Niila and I often discussed whether our rock music could be regarded as knapsu. The word is Tornedalen Finnish and means something like 'unmanly', something that only women do. You could say that in Tornedalen the male role boils down to just one thing: not being knapsu. That sounds simple and obvious, but it is complicated by various special rules that can often take decades to learn, something that the men who come up north from Southern Sweden often come up against. Certain activities are basically knapsu and hence should be avoided by men. Changing curtains, for instance; knitting, weaving carpets, milking by hand, watering the houseplants and that sort of thing. Other occupations are definitely manly, such as tree-felling, elk hunting, building log cabins, floating logs downriver, and fighting on dance floors. The world has been split in two since time immemorial and everybody knew the score.*
>
> *But then came welfare. And suddenly there were lots of new activities and occupations that confused the concepts. As the knapsu concept had developed over many*

hundreds of years, as subconscious processes in the minds of generations, the definitions could no longer keep up. Except in certain areas. Engines, for instance, are manly. Petrol engines are more manly than electric ones. Cars, snowmobiles and power saws are therefore not knapsu. But can a man sew with a sewing machine? Whip cream with an electric mixer? Milk cows with a milking machine? Empty a dishwasher? Can a real man vacuum-clean his car and still retain his dignity? Those are some questions for you to think about. It's even more difficult when it comes to new trends. For instance is it knapsu to eat reduced-fat margarine? To have a heater in your car? To buy hair gel? To meditate? To swim using a snorkel? To use sticking plaster? To put dog poo in a plastic bag? (16)

> **Reflection**
>
> Can you think of ambiguous practices such as the ones in the extract? In your context, what forms of work and other social practices have shifted in how they have been gendered?
> Does the nation state you live in have a gender identity? If so where does this come from?
> How does the list of questions presented by the author relate to the exercise *Gender Boxes*?

1.3.4 Gender and sexuality

'Sexuality' is another complex term in this discussion, as it simultaneously refers to (a) reproduction, (b) erotic desire for another human being, and (c) a central aspect of gender identity.

Because of the relationship between heterosexual sex and reproduction, sexuality is often seen as having a natural relationship with stable male and female roles. However there is much more to sexuality than that: search for a book on sexuality on any internet book shop and you will find titles relating to physiology, psychology, culture, morals and ethics, history, organised religion and spirituality. Sexuality and sexual identities vary across time, and sexuality has always been important in addressing the nature and limits of human freedom.

The debate between 'essentialist ideas' (that argue for definite biological differences between men and women) and 'constructivist ideas' (that emphasise the fundamental influences of society and culture on gendered identities) is also an important one in relation to sexuality. The idea that sexuality is a purely natural state is an ambiguous one: on the one hand, as section 2.2 examines, crimes against women have often been 'explained' in terms of the essential sex drive of men. Similarly fixed ideas of gender and sexuality have been important to the heterosexual norms characteristic of patriarchy: for example, it is only recently in many countries that rape between married people has been seen as a crime (see section 1.4). Most obviously, the idea that biological reproduction fixes 'normal' sexual identities acts as the basis for discrimination against sexual identities that are thus seen to be different and abnormal (see section 1.5.2 on the political response to this of Lesbian, Gay, Bisexual and Transgendered activists).

The idea of fixed categories of sexuality, just like the idea of unchanging, essential gender identities, is undermined by histories of sexuality that show changing practices and values attached to forms of sexual behaviour between people. One of the most famous of these is the work of the French philosopher Michel Foucault in his three volume *History of Sexuality*. In volume 1, for instance, he shows that before 'homosexuality' became categorised as a form of sexual identity in the nineteenth century, sexual relations between men were regarded in different contexts as an act that may be celebrated or punished, *but did not define the identities of those involved*.

The main point, perhaps, is not that youth workers and leaders have to solve a long-running debate between biology and culture, but rather to bear in mind that sexuality, as with gender, is something that involves enormous diversity, yet is always disciplined to some extent by social practices and expectations.

1.3.5 Gender and inequality

What is meant by patriarchy? Are women inferior or superior to men?

The introduction to GENDER MATTERS argued that it is our view that gender has been a neglected topic in youth work in Europe in recent years. If this is the case, it is a serious neglect that needs to be addressed:

> *Marking the twenty-fifth anniversary of the adoption of the Convention to Eliminate All Forms of Discrimination Against Women (CEDAW), the UN Committee for CEDAW announced that no country in the world has achieved full equality between men and women in law and in practice. The Deputy Secretary-General Louis Frechette asserted that women are still "significantly under-represented in public life," and still suffer from violence and sexual harassment in their daily lives, reports UN News Service.* [17]

As the next sections will discuss, this kind of thinking on gender has emerged from different periods of struggle, primarily by women and sexual minorities, for equal rights and possibilities, and also for a proper critique of the way in which power works in most societies. A key aim of gender analysis and politics has been to examine the ways in which masculine power, privileges and dominance have been normalised in public and private spheres, and, as we shall see in chapter two, how this has devastating links to violence.

There have been many different models and theories offered for capturing how men have predominantly placed themselves and been placed in social hierarchy over women. The idea of 'patriarchy' is often used as a kind of shorthand for male dominance, and it has also been the subject of more specific theories. In general, patriarchy describes the way in which gender roles and possibilities have tended to subordinate women to men. Patriarchy involves the acceptance of fundamental ideas about the nature and value of women, their roles – including heterosexual norms of wife and mother – and their possibilities, and these ideas tend to be based on appeals to biological reasoning: women are more naturally suited to be carers, for example. Some discussions of patriarchy argue that it is dependent on the divisions in labour that have tended to dominate in industrial capitalist societies. In other words, the predominance of men at work in the public sphere, and women working in the private to 'make the home' has deeply influenced the durability of traditional gender roles. However it is important to recognise that this is not the whole story, as it does not take account of the role of women in the work force of industrial societies, nor of the many changes that have taken place in work-gender roles in societies where heavy industry has been replaced by service and information industries.

> **Reflection**
>
> *The reasonable man…*
> In many legal systems an idea of 'the reasonable man' has been used as a hypothetical measure to help juries to reach their decisions. They may be asked to imagine, 'How would a reasonable man act under these circumstances?' In some instances, the explicit reference to a man has been replaced with a 'reasonable person'.
>
> Have you come across this idea in your context? Does it exist in some shape or form?
> Does changing the name change the imagination behind it, in your opinion?

Chapter 2 continues this examination by looking at gendered inequality and types of violence.

1.4 Masculinities

When we examine the ways in which gender relations have privileged men as the centre of rationality and normality, it may come as no surprise that it has taken quite a while for masculinity to be understood as a process of gender construction rather than just a way of describing how men are. Indeed the title of this section – masculinities – acknowledges that there is not just one interpretation for 'a man' to demonstrate he is 'a man'; masculinity varies across socio-cultural contexts and within groups and networks, and different men, with different experiences, relationships and pressures may perform their masculinity differently and inconsistently. As Whitehead and Barrett explain,

> *Masculinities are those behaviours, languages and practices, existing in specific cultural and organisational locations, which are commonly associated with men and thus culturally defined as not feminine.* [18]

In using the plural masculinities, this quotation emphasises that there is no one coherent set of expectations surrounding 'manhood'. Indeed, one of the reasons for the rise of studies of masculinity has been the change in traditional masculine roles in post-industrial societies. Nevertheless, while increasing attention is paid to the ways in which masculinity has been pluralized in certain contexts during recent decades, it must be stressed, particularly in a publication analysing gender-based violence, that the pressure and expectation to behave in terms of dominant codes of masculinity remains a prevalent experience for many men, with consequences for women, children and men in turn.

Cultural expectations of male behaviour, as the quotation above suggests, often centre on differentiating masculinity from the realm of femininity, where homosexuality is cast as having a particular relationship to femininity. Masculine identities, like all identities, are forged in difference and association: being a man involves not being something other than man and being like certain other men. Masculinity, seen in different contexts, involves displaying attitudes and behaviours that signify and validate male identities in relation to each other, and being recognised in particular ways by other men and women.

R.W Connell, in his book *Masculinities* (1995), argues that masculinity exists and shifts within networks of gender relationships. He argues against notions of masculinity that accept normative standards for what men *should* be like, against essentialist accounts of central male characteristics, as well as against accounts of masculinity that focus on describing differences. Instead, he argues, what is important to a meaningful analysis of gender and masculinity is the "…processes and relationships through which men and women conduct gendered lives. 'Masculinity', to the extent the term can be briefly defined at all, is simultaneously a place in gender relations, the practices through which men and women engage that place in gender, and the effects of these practices in bodily experience, personality and culture". [19]

He provides the useful idea of multiple masculinities. Notice how in this next quotation different conceptualisations of 'masculine sexuality' are revealed to be historically context specific:

> *Different cultures, and different periods of history, construct masculinity differently. For instance, some cultures make heroes of soldiers, and regard violence as the ultimate test of masculinity; others look at soldiering with disdain and regard violence as contemptible. Some cultures regard homosexual sex as incompatible with true masculinity; others think no-one can be a real man without having had homosexual relationships. It follows that in large-scale multicultural societies there are likely to be multiple definitions of masculinity…There are, for instance, differences in the expression of masculinity between Latino and Anglo men in the United States, and between Greek or Lebanese and Anglo boys in Australia. Other recent research looks at the different ways in which majority and minority youth may express their masculinity through popular culture in French, German and Dutch cities. The meaning of masculinity in working-class life is different from the meaning in middle-class life, not to mention among the very rich and the very poor. Equally important, more than one kind of masculinity can be found within a given cultural setting. Within any workplace,*

neighbourhood or peer group, there are likely to be different understandings of masculinity. [20]

Connell argues that it is important to consider the power relationships between different masculinities as well as their relationships with femininities, and to analyse how this socially reproduces, supports or challenges the distribution of power between women and men. These categories are not rigid types and have been subject to some criticism, so they are best regarded as fluid yet useful indicators:

'Hegemonic masculinities': These masculinities are highly visible, respected and in a position of authority in relation to other masculinities in a particular setting. They may not be the most widespread form, but they are likely to be those most admired and represent standards for others. Examples might include decisive business leaders, popular boys in their school peer group and certain sportsmen and what they seem to 'embody'. Hegemonic masculinities can be seen as dominant in the entire gender order.

'Complicit masculinities': To be complicit means to condone or support something without being actively engaged in it. Complicit masculinities are those that benefit in general from the social dominance of men while not actively seeking to oppress women. A complicit action would be, for example, to deny the existence of inequality or other problems, or merely not to question the way in which gender relations are generally ordered. This complicity may not be coherent across a range of issues, and the degree to which most men display some form of complicity is a subject of intense debate.

'Subordinate masculinities' are those that are culturally placed as inferior – homosexuality in relation to heterosexuality is an obvious example – or those that have made a conscious effort to protest and 'exit' from hegemonic and complicit positions. Other subordinate masculinities may involve those whose physical appearance does not conform to standards set by hegemonic embodiments. In relation to homosexuality, this formulation challenges the normative assumption that homosexuality is close to 'femininity'.

'Marginalised masculinities' are those that are placed as different by issues of class, ethnicity or status. They may display and enjoy masculine power in certain contexts, but are always ultimately related to the hegemonic norms and images.

1.4.1 Case study: The context of young men's lives in Northern Ireland

In the following case study, Ken Harland, who has worked extensively as a youth worker and researcher in Belfast with young men and the issue of masculinities, considers issues young men face in their everyday lives. This case study deals with issues addressed in his book Young Men Talking (1997). [21]

Reflection on any aspect of life in Northern Ireland must be considered within the context of the conflict that has been prevalent for almost 35 years. Since 1969, Northern Ireland has witnessed widespread social, economic and political upheaval through what is commonly known as 'the troubles.' Throughout this period cultural and political identity has been fiercely disputed with young people developing their sense of ethnic identity "in the midst of political crisis and sectarian confrontation".[22] Sectarianism and the effects of the troubles have been shown to have a significant influence upon young people growing up in Northern Ireland. Connolly and Maginn [23] found that sectarianism amongst children in Northern Ireland was rooted in their day to day experiences, and that by the age of three, children had not only developed an understanding of the categories of 'Protestant' and 'Catholic,' but were also able to apply negative characteristics from one to the other. As young men grow up these negative perceptions not only increase but are also exacerbated by other important factors. For example, in my inner city Belfast study, the young men perceived schools and local communities as hostile environments where they increasingly felt apathetic, vulnerable and disillusioned. The young men were wary of other young males within their community whilst fearful of young men from different traditions. Paramilitary violence was a constant threat that resulted in the young men feeling suspicious and confused, particularly regarding issues surrounding law and order.

Young Men's 'contradictory' experience of Masculinity

Issues surrounding masculinity and what it means to be a man are increasingly complex, contradictory and confusing. From childhood males are bombarded with powerful messages about what it means to be a man. Most boys learn to act in a particular way, displaying aggressive forms of masculine behaviour and avoiding behaviours that may be considered effeminate. For many young males, the consequences of failing to live up to accepted standards of masculinity is to risk losing their masculine status, which can have disastrous effects upon male health and self-esteem. Through their association with local interpretations of masculinity and femininity, many young men in working class areas of Northern Ireland learn to exist and survive within a complex and contradictory web of masculine thoughts and beliefs. One outcome of this is that young men believe they must deny, or conceal, important aspects of their personality in order to display their masculinity, believing it is by 'acting tough' that men get status and respect. The young men in my study believed men should be powerful, strong, brave, intelligent, healthy, sexy, mature and in control of every aspect of their lives. In reality however, their lives were full of 'contradictions' because most young men felt powerless, feared the threat of daily violence, were labelled 'stupid' at school, did not pay attention to their health needs and specifically their mental health, did not have much sexual experience, had not been in any type of sexual relationship and felt they were perceived by adults as 'immature.' Appreciating these 'contradictions' is important to understanding internal pressures that many young males feel in regard to how they construct their masculine identity and what it means to be a man. Contradictions between young men's perceived power and their sense of powerlessness capture what Connell (1995) calls 'protest masculinity,' whereby boys make claims to power when there are no real resources for doing so. In my study, the young men's perceptions of masculinity resulted in them being dismissive of their pain and separated from their internal world of feelings and emotions, often to the extent that they appeared 'unemotional.' Significant socio-economic changes brought about as a result of de-industrialisation, uncertain youth-to-adult transitions, the perceived threat of violence and the changing position of women in society are all contributory factors with regard to young men's masculine expectations being full of complex contradictions.

Young men and risk taking behaviour

Clinging to stereotypical images of men and masculinity encourages young men to willingly jeopardise their health through engaging in high-risk activities. A key finding in my research with these young men revealed that because they were ambivalent about their masculinity, they felt enormous pressure to *prove* their masculinity to others. Subsequently, they were prepared to take risks as part of the price that young men pay in the pursuit of manhood. The notion of risk is a recurring theme in young men's health statistics. This is evidenced by male risk-taking behaviours such as driving without a seat belt, eating snack foods, fighting, street violence, not visiting doctors, alcohol abuse, car theft, young men internalising their problems and increased suicide rates. Whilst the young men were aware of the dangers, they perceived risk-taking as a necessary component of male youth culture and as an important way in which males demonstrate their masculinity to others.

Public and Private – the 'two worlds' of young men

In contemporary western societies it is becoming more commonplace for men to be criticised rather than praised for their ability to withhold emotions. Increasingly, men who withhold emotions are accused of being 'out of touch with their emotions' or 'out of touch with their feminine side'. Thirty years ago such accusations were not deemed necessary or incorporated into gender analysis. Prior to this, it was generally accepted that women were more emotional than men and therefore when women publicly displayed their feelings this was accepted as evidence of their femininity. It was taken for granted that women were 'better' at expressing their emotional needs than men. Conversely, men who could restrain their emotions were perceived as exemplary role models within traditional interpretations of masculinity.

The young men in question experienced ambivalence between their 'public' and 'private' persona. In 'public' the young men felt enormous pressure to appear confident (often to the point of machismo) and evidence their masculinity to others in a forceful way, typically through the use of insults and bravado. In public the young men feared being humiliated by appearing weak (or feminine), which was threatening to their sense of male pride. Subsequently, it was in 'private' that these young men faced their anxieties and tried to cope with their fears and inner emotions. They learned that 'real men' should be in control and are therefore reluctant to seek support from others. Major difficulties lie in the fact that in traditional masculine cultures there are no realistic mechanisms to encourage young men to seek support or become more skilled at expressing their emotions.

1.5 Politics of gender: movements for a more equal society

1.5.1 Women's movements

The idea of the 'women's movement' seems relatively new: when asked about it most people might say that it started in the late 19th century with the fight for the right to vote. Equally, it may be widely felt that women now have equal political, social and even equal human rights as men, so there is not much point to such a movement. Neither of these positions is accurate. Therefore, what is the women's movement, when did it start and why is it still relevant? There have always been outstanding, extraordinary women such as Jeanne D'Arc or Elizabeth I, who played an important role in local or world history, but they were not advocates of women's issues. The women's movement is made up of women and men who work and fight *to improve the lives of women as a social group*. Until recently in most societies women were confined to the home as daughters, wives and mothers, and in a majority of cases we only know about women's lives if they were related to some famous men. That is why the organised women's movement started in the 19th century, even though women's activism was probably always present in human societies.

One of the early pioneers who thought and wrote about women as a group is the Italian writer Christine de Pizan, who published a book about women's situation as early as 1495. She writes about the books she read by famous men who questioned whether women are human beings at all or more similar to animals, and wrote books about the sins and weaknesses of girls and women. She is a great example of the early stage of the struggle for women's equality, but her situation was very special: she could read and write, which was very unusual for a woman at that time. Later, women took part in the activities of the French revolution from the very beginning: the demonstrations that led to the revolution started with a large group of working women marching to Versailles to demand not only food to feed their families but also political change. However, when the revolution was over, women's rights were taken off the agenda, and when Napoleon's rule started women were sent back home, devoid of economic, social and political equality.

The women's movement started to reach more people in North America, mostly because there women were allowed to go to school earlier than in Europe, and women who can read, write and are encouraged to think for themselves usually start to question how society works. The first activists travelled around North America and fought for the end of both slavery and women's oppression. They organised the 'First Women's Rights Convention' in 1848, and continued to campaign to improve the social position of all women. The movement also began in Europe for the same purposes: activists collected signatures demanding that working women should receive their own wages and not their husbands', that women should be able to own a house and have custody of their children.

The fight for women's right to vote in elections is known as the 'suffrage movement'. By the end of the 19th century it had become a worldwide movement, and the words 'feminism' and 'feminist movement' have also been used since then. This first wave of feminist activism included mass demonstrations, the publishing of newspapers, organised debates and the forming of international women's organisations. Partly as a result, by the 1920s, women had won the right to vote in most of Western Europe and North America. At the same time women became active in socialist and social democratic parties because more and more women started to work outside the home in factories and offices. Women were first allowed to go to university in the early 20th century, since when more and more women have had a career as well as a family. The feminist movement was banned in countries where fascist parties gained power, and women started organising again after the end of the Second World War. At this time women gained equal political rights in several Eastern European countries, and women's emancipation was an important aim in these societies: most women were allowed to take on full-time jobs, divorce their husbands and go to university. However, as all aspects of life in this part of Europe were controlled by communist parties, women's emancipation was not achieved in reality, and there was not a real women's movement until the collapse of the Soviet bloc in 1989.

In Western Europe and the USA on the other hand, the feminist women's movement was resurgent by the 1970s. Although this *second wave of feminist activism* aimed to achieve 'women's liberation,' different groups wanted to do it in different ways. *Liberal feminists* wanted better equality laws and reforms of social institutions such as schools, churches and the media. *Radical feminists* argued that the cause of women's inequality is *patriarchy*: men, as a group, oppress women. They also focused on men's violence against women, and started to talk about violence in the family, and rape. Socialist feminists say that it is combination of patriarchy and capitalism that causes women's oppression. The second wave of feminism also resulted in new areas of science: women's studies became a discipline which can be studied at university, and books have been published about women's achievements in literature, music, science and women's previously unwritten history. Finally, the women's movement played an important role in the writing of international documents about women's rights such as the Universal Declaration of Human Rights and the Convention on the Elimination of all Forms of Discrimination Against Women (CEDAW).

1.5.2 Lesbian, Gay, Bisexual and Transgendered (LGBT) Movements

What are the gender issues confronting the LGBT movement and LGBT people, and how have they changed over time?

Same sex relationships have always existed, but the roots of organised LGBT movements in Europe and the USA can be traced back to the 1920s and 1930s and the development of an urban gay and lesbian subculture.[24] For example, Berlin was famous for its gay subculture. Homosexual organisations began to develop after the Second World War. In the Netherlands in 1946 gay men, and later lesbian women, got together under the nickname 'The Shakespeare Club' and later as an organisation called C.O.C. The name meant Centre for Culture and Leisure, a reminder of the pseudonym the organisation initially adopted after its foundation. C.O.C. is known as the oldest Lesbian, Gay, Bisexual and Transgender organisation in the world.

In the USA, the first attempts to set up a lesbian and gay organisation can be traced back to 1950 in Los Angeles, when a small group of men set up the Mattachine Society. Mostly male in membership, it was joined in 1955 by a lesbian organization in San Francisco, the Daughters of Bilitis. In the 1950s these organizations remained small, but they established chapters in several cities and published magazines that were a beacon of hope to the readers.

The beginning of a gay political movement is now often traced back to 27th June, 1969, and a raid by the New York City police on a Greenwich Village gay bar, The Stonewall Inn. Contrary to expectations, the patrons fought back, provoking three nights of rioting in the area accompanied by the appearance of 'gay power' slogans on the buildings. Almost overnight, a massive grassroots gay liberation movement was born. Owing much to the radical protest of African-Americans, women, and anti-war protesters of the 1960s, gays challenged all forms of hostility and punishment meted out by society. Choosing to 'come out of the closet' and publicly proclaim their identity, they provided a movement for social change with substantial impetus. In general the same developments can be seen in Western European countries, where the lesbian and gay world is no longer an underground subculture but, in larger cities in particular, is a well-organized community. This often involves gay businesses, political clubs, social service agencies, community centres and religious congregations bringing people together. In a number of places, openly gay candidates run for elections.

During these struggles, homosexual men and lesbian women came to realise that they did not and would not conform to dominant social gender roles. Homosexuals not only challenged the heterosexual norm but also challenged the images of how men and women should behave, what they should look like and what roles they should fulfil in society. These confrontations with repressive social norms have been carried out in spectacular ways that have increased visibility, such as a 'kiss–in' of lesbians on a German town square, and sometimes through mainstream political approaches such as lobbying and advocacy. Publicly 'out' lesbians and gays in politics and organisations as the International Lesbian and Gay Association (ILGA) and the International Lesbian, Gay, Bisexual and Transgender Youth and Students Organisation (IGLYO) have and continue to contribute to the inclusion of LGBT issues in discussions on equal opportunities, human rights and general social policy.

> *The previous section on feminism, and the following section on men's groups, point out that other movements have played a role in the LGBT struggle. In particular, the feminist movement's de-linking of sexuality and procreation, its critique of marriage, and dominant male-female role patterns have contributed to opening a social space for the experiences and identities of gay men and women. However, this does not imply that either struggle has been exhausted: gender politics do not progress in a*

straight line, and rigid gender expectations still cause significant marginalisation on the basis of sexual identity. Moreover, there has been a backlash by social conservatives against both feminism and the LBGT movement. Even a few years ago, when Rosanne kissed a lesbian on the US television show Rosanne, there was a huge outcry. The American Family Association (AFA) condemned ABC television for allowing such show of affection on TV. Tim Wildmon, the Vice President of the AFA said, "The television industry continues to push the homosexual agenda with increasing fervency, with regular homosexual characters, same-sex marriages, and now passionate lesbian kissing scenes. And they won't stop their assault on morality until American society cries 'Uncle!' and fully accepts the homosexual lifestyle as legitimate." [25]

Reflection

How is homosexuality represented in television programmes in your context? What stereotypes exist? Are there any representations that challenge these stereotypes? Is there a public debate such as the one described above in the USA?

Despite the fact that in several countries in Europe legal changes have resulted in anti-discrimination legislation and same sex partnerships, or 'civil marriage', the social acceptance of LGBTs is still far from unconditional and secure. For example, the writers of this manual have observed that LBGT issues remain something of a taboo even among 'progressives' in the human rights movement and in European youth work. It should also be pointed out that one cannot speak of *the* LBGT movement. Although lesbians, gays, bisexuals and transgenders are usually mentioned as one category, there remain many differences between them and within these broad sexual identities. Sometimes LBGTs work closely together, and at other times separate campaigns and strategies are pursued. *Within* the LGBT movement a wide variety of attitudes towards political demands and gender expectations can be found. 'How homosexuals should behave' is a constant discussion topic, shifting between approaches which aim for greater mainstream acceptability, and more radical identity politics that play with images of (fe)male identities.

1.5.3 Men's Groups and Boys' Groups

In this section, Jeff Hearn, Professor at the Swedish School of Economics in Helsinki and the University of Huddersfield, discusses anti-sexist men's groups and activities. He first set up such a group in 1978 and since 1999 he has been part of 'profeministimiehet' (pro-feminist men) in Helsinki, Finland.

Have you ever wondered what it would be like to sit with a group of boys or men, but without a prearranged reason, agenda or diversion? What would you talk about? What would you do?

Boys and men often meet, socialise and organise in groups, and often seem to like doing so very much indeed. Many of these groups are either boys-only or men-only or clearly dominated by boys or men. Such groups can be found in schools and other places of education, at work, in sport, in pubs and clubs or on the street. They are places and spaces for men and boys to meet others of the same gender. But they are often *not* called men's groups or boys' groups, even when they clearly are. Sometimes these groups are specifically organised as such, as for example, with many single-sex sports; sometimes they are coupled with formal or organised attempts to exclude girls and women, such as men-only clubs or rooms; often they are taken-for-granted as "just the way things are" in, for example, some leading management groups or 'expert' panel discussions or street gangs; sometimes they seem, by chance, to "just happen …"; and of course sometimes they are gay groups.

Most of these groups are not what I would call *explicitly gender-conscious*. They are not usually meeting together to consciously reflect on their gender as boys and / or men, or on their own explicit gender interests in relation to women. However, for some time now, boys and men are gathering, more or less gender-consciously, to talk about and reflect on their own gender. Since the 1970s there have been a number of forms of explicitly gender-conscious groups and politics by men and boys, from anti-feminist to *pro-feminist*[3]. Anti-sexist men's groups in the 1970s and 1980s, influenced by feminist, gay, left, anarchist and green politics, were active in national and regional conferences, gatherings and campaigns. One list of 'Anti-sexist men's commitments' produced in 1980 ran:

- Commitment to the (anti-sexist) group
- Consciousness-raising done rigorously
- Support for the women's liberation movement
- Support for gay liberation
- Sharing childcare
- Learning from feminist and gay culture
- Action on our own behalf
- Propaganda and outreach programmes (linked to action)
- Link-ups with other men against sexism groups
- Renunciation of violence (physical, emotional and verbal) [26]

By the mid-1980s, in the UK at least, there was a loss of momentum in the anti-sexist men's movement, and many activists either left or tried to bring these issues into more main-

---

3 What is pro-feminism? Pro-feminism describes men's solidarity and support for feminist struggles and issues. Just as there are various feminisms so there are various forms of pro feminism. However, amongst all the different viewpoints, pro-feminists share a conviction to listen to and learn from feminism and women, and to rethink and deconstruct male gender as the dominant and hegemonic gender. This involves actively changing both ourselves and other men – personally, politically, at home, at work, in the media, campaigns, law, and so on. Examples of men's actions and power that need changing include men's violence, sexual harassment, gender discrimination, sexism and patriarchal dominance more generally. Pro-feminist organising can include campaigns, demonstrations, posters, flyers, writing letters, articles and pamphlets, producing T-shirts, postcards etc., as well as more personally orientated activities, including consciousness-raising groups.

stream and professional work in teaching, youth work, welfare, journalism, broadcasting, therapy, consultancy, writing and research. This was partly a case of putting these ideas into effect but also sometimes of diluting them. The movement towards mythopoetic groups followed, groups that tried to 'reclaim' authentic, essential masculine identities. More recently, organisations for men's rights and fathers' rights have become more visible and active in spectacular ways, even though men and fathers have had privileged gender rights for a very long time.

There are thus many different motivations for meeting in gender-conscious men's groups or boys' groups. They can range from being actively in favour of gender equality and feminism to being actively hostile to gender equality and feminism – reinforcing and returning to the old, traditional, patriarchal ways. There is a kind of continuum from those men who are actively supportive of gender equality and feminism towards those who are in favour of this in theory but do not do anything in particular, to those who are 'not bothered' and on to those who are actively hostile.

Another way of understanding these groups is in terms of different positions within three points of a triangle: first, recognition of institutionalised privileges; second, recognition of differences / inequalities among men, and, third, recognition of the 'costs of masculinity'. This model shows the complexity of motivations, especially regarding the different kinds of differences / inequalities amongst men. It highlights how one cannot reduce gender politics to one continuum, but rather opens up some personal and political spaces. These various positions can be occupied by individual men, groups of men, whole organizations and even whole governments; they can operate in gender equality politics, in working life, at home, in personal relationships, or even in bed.

There has recently been a revival of interest in pro-feminist organising, at least in a European and international context. Examples include the European Pro-feminist Network[27], the pro-feminist project *Ending Gender-based Violence*[28] (supported by UNICEF and the Swedish development agency, SIDA, the EU Critical Research on Men in Europe which is explicitly (pro)feminist[29], and the International Network for the Radical Critique of Masculinities. There is growing interest from governments, the EU and UN in the contribution of men to gender equality. The UN Division for the Advancement of Women has promoted 'The role of men and boys in achieving gender equality'.[30] This theme is also one of the social priorities of the Finnish government.

Nevertheless, there are still ambiguities in many discussions about men, boys and gender equality: these relate to whether it is gender-conscious groups or more generally, how men can contribute to women's struggles for gender equality, and about what men can gain from gender equality? Sadly, it tends usually to be the latter. To put this another way: can gender equality be achieved within the context of patriarchy? If not, then patriarchy needs to be abolished, hence the need for boys and men to be anti-patriarchal and pro-feminist, not simply taking part in gender equality debates.

If you are thinking of starting, or planning to start or facilitate a group, you need firstly to think about what kind of group it is, and what its purpose is. Is it for consciousness-raising, discussion, therapy, writing or activism? Is it a self-help group, or is it to be led or facilitated? Find out and contact those you know who might be interested. Ask if they know others who might be interested. Think also about your and others' personal and political motives for doing this. This is especially important if you advertise a first meeting publicly. If you do, maybe it's good to have at least two people facilitating the meeting, rather than it being 'chaired' by just one. There are many obvious issues for such groups to address: being a boy, growing up, mothers and fathers, brothers and sisters, women, other men, intimacy, sex and sexuality, violence, sport, fear, your / men's bodies, emotions, work, love, politics or the media, or try something more specific, for example, hair, shoes, shaving, trousers, meat, photos, computer games or fruit.

Meeting and sitting down together, perhaps without even a fixed reason or excuse (such as drinking or smoking or playing some sport) may seem, at first, very weird, or even very embarrassing. But others are probably feeling the same. You'll get used to it. One of the things to look at is the fair use of time in groups. A simple way is to begin and end with 'rounds' in a circle where everyone can talk uninterrupted in turn, but for no longer than, for example, two minutes.

A simple, but often very revealing, exercise is for the boys or men in the group, either on their own or in pairs or sub-groups to address three questions:
- What do you like about being a man / boy?
- What do you not like?
- What things would you like to change, and how?

This often involves recognising dilemmas and ambivalences. Key questions include:
- How important is changing myself and other men?
- How much effort should I put into this?
- Do I want this to be a fundamental part of my life?
- In what ways do I feel ambivalent about change?

There are often contradictions in seeking to change:
- How do I recognise 'being a man' without emphasising that status?
- How do I recognise 'being a man' whilst stopping being a man?
- Do I need to depend more on men, on women or on both?
- How do I learn from feminism? What do I mean by feminism?
- How do I learn from feminism without taking over women's space?

There is also a need to act consciously in groups. Common pitfalls in groups include:
- 'hogging the show'- not giving space to others
- being the continual problem-solver
- defensiveness

- task and content focus to the exclusion of nurturing
- negativism
- using formal power positions
- stubbornness and dogmatism
- listening only to oneself
- avoiding feelings
- condescension and paternalism
- using sexuality to manipulate women
- seeking attention and support from women while running the show
- protectively storing key group information for one's own use
- speaking for others [31]

It is important to recognise that common forms of control are unacceptable. These include yelling, threatening gestures, verbal threats, defining reality unilaterally, withholding positive attention, persistent criticism, ridiculing, and demeaning women. Responsible action for men and boys involves:

- limiting our talking time to our fair share
- not interrupting who is speaking
- becoming a good listener
- getting and giving support
- not giving answers and solutions
- relaxing
- not speaking on every subject
- not putting others down
- nurturing democratic group processes
- interrupting others' oppressive behaviour [32]

A key challenge throughout is to change men's and boys' relations with both women and girls, and with each other. How is it that heterosexual men and boys are often so 'homosocial': preferring, valuing and choosing men, boys and male company over women, girls and female company? Oddly, such heterosexual homosociality can sometimes go together with homophobia. This is an aspect of men's and boys' relations with each other that needs to be strongly challenged.

Endnotes for Chapter 1

(1) Source: www.who.int/gender/whatisgender
(2) Menon-Sen, K. (1998). *Moving From Policy to Practice: A Gender Mainstreaming Strategy for UNDP India.* UNDP.
(3) Pilcher, J. & Whelehan, I. (2004). *50 Key Concepts in Gender Studies.* London: Sage. (p.82).
(4) Source: http://www.emich.edu/lgbtrc/resources/files/lgbt-definitions.pdf
(5) Hartley, J. (1994). 'Gender' in O'Sullivan, T. et al. *Key Concepts in Communication and Cultural Studies* London: Routledge. (p.127).
(6) Edgar, A. & Sedgwick, P. (Eds.). (1999). *Key Concepts in Cultural Theory.* London: Routledge. (p.158).
(7) Alsop, R., Fitzsimons, A. & Lennon, K. (2002). *Theorising Gender,* Oxford: Polity. (p.5).
(8) Hart, K. (2003). 'Studying World Society' in Eriksen, T.H. (Ed.) *Globalisation.* London: Pluto. (p.217).
(9) Bauman, Z. & May, T. (2001). *Thinking Sociologically.* London: Blackwell Publishing. (p.17)
(10) Ibid.
(11) Ibid. (p.7)
(12) Pilcher, J. & Whelehan, I. op.cit. (p7).
(13) Source: http://education.qld.gov.au/students/advocacy/equity/gender-sch/issues/gender-under.html
(14) Alsop, R. et al, op.cit. (p.3).
(15) Pilcher, J. & Whelehan, I. op.cit. (p.59).
(16) Niemi, M. (2004). *Popular Music,* New York: Seven Stories Press. (p.11-12).
(17) Feminist Daily News Wire, (2004).www.feminist.org/news/newsbyte/uswirestory.asp?id=8693
(18) Whitehead, S.M., & Barrett, F.J. (Eds.). (2001). *The Masculinities Reader.* Oxford: Polity Press.
(19) Connell, R.W. (1995). *Masculinities.* Berkeley: University of California Press. (p.71).
(20) Source: http://toolkit.endabuse.org/Resources/UnderstandingMen
(21) Hartland, K. (1997). *Young men talking: Voices from Belfast (Advocacy Series)*, London: Working With Men
(22) Bell, Desmond 1990. *Acts of union. Youth culture and sectarianism in Northern Ireland.* London: Macmillan
(23) Connolly, P. & Maginn, P. (1999). *Sectarianism, Children and Community Relations in Northern Ireland.* Coleraine: University of Ulster. (p.97).
(24) Tielman, R. (1982). *Homoseksualiteit in Nederland.* Amsterdam, Meppel: Boom.
(25) Press release from the **American Family Association,** (AFA) a Fundamentalist Christian anti-homosexual group, 1997, Jan.14. http://www.religioustolerance.org/hom_0020.htm
(26) Commitments Collective (1980) Anti-sexist commitments for men – draught [*sic.*] 3. *Anti-Sexist Men's Newsletter,* 9, 17.
(27) http://www.europrofem.org/
(28) http://www.sida.se/content/1/c6/02/47/27/SVI34602.pdf)
(29) http://www.cromenet.org
(30) http://www.un.org/womenwatch/daw/egm/men-boys2003/
(31) Moyer, B. & Tuttle, A. (1983). *Off Their Backs ... and on Our Own Two Feet.* Philadelphia: New Society Publishers. (pp.24-29).
(32) Ibid.

2. Gender-based violence

2.1 Introduction

What is the difference between violence against women and gender-based violence?

'Gender-based violence' (GBV) is still an emerging and developing term. Originally it was used mostly to replace the term '(male) violence against women', because the word woman refers to both individuals of the female sex and to feminine gender roles in society. Those developing the term wanted to emphasize that violence against women is a phenomenon that is related to the gender of *both* victim and perpetrator. Many definitions continue to focus solely on the fact that women are victims of violence: for example, the UNHCHR's CEDAW (Convention to Eliminate All Forms of Discrimination Against Women) committee states that GBV is "…violence that is directed against a woman because she is a woman or that affects women disproportionately".

However, there is a development towards extending this definition to all forms of violence that are related to (a) social expectations and social positions based on gender and (b) not conforming to a socially accepted gender-role. In this way gender-based violence is increasingly a term that connects all acts of violence rooted in some form of 'patriarchal ideology' (see 1.4), and can thus be committed against both women and men by women and men with the purpose of maintaining social power for (heterosexual) men. This evolution of the definition can be observed in the following description:

> *Gender-based violence is an umbrella term for any harm that is perpetrated against a person's will; that has a negative impact on the physical or psychological health, development, and identity of the person; and that is the result of gendered power inequities that exploit distinctions between males and females, among males, and among females. Although not exclusive to women and girls, GBV principally affects them across all cultures. Violence may be physical, sexual, psychological, economic, or sociocultural. Categories of perpetrators may include family members, community members, and those acting on behalf of or in proportion to the disregard of cultural, religious, state, or intra-state institutions.* [1]

This table summarises the issues addressed in the quotation above:

Gender based violence	
What ?	Action restricting a person's will or freedom Negative impact on physical or psychological health Negative impact on the identity of a person Exploits distinctions between male and female, among males, and among females
Against whom ?	Everyone, but it affects mainly girls and women
How ?	Violence may be: • physical • sexual • psychological • economic • sociocultural
Who does it ?	Everyone can. Common perpetrators may include: • family members • community members • those acting on behalf of cultural, religious, state, or intra-state institutions, or free to act because of their disregard

Perpetrators benefit in different ways when committing acts of violence. There are two main functions of gender-based violence:

- In the case of women in general, gender-based violence is a way of assuring women's inferior position in society. Violence against women, and the threat of it, is a form of gender-based violence that deprives women of their rights socially before the law becomes involved. This is one of the reasons why long-standing laws on equality of the sexes, or general legal sanctions for most forms of violence against women, have not been able to end or even significantly limit the inequality of women and men by themselves. [2]
- In the case of LGBT (Lesbian, Gay, Bisexual and Transgendered) people and men who do not act according to dominant masculine gender roles, gender-based violence has the function of correction by example. The severity of the 'punishment' for men who do not act according to the demands of male gender roles (whether gay, bisexual or heterosexual) may be related to the perceived danger that their difference presents to normalised and dominant assumptions about gender. Their very lives might collide and appear to contradict the idea that there are natural forms of behaviour and social roles in general for men and women.

2.2 What is violence?

Can victims provoke violence? Should perpetrators of violence always be punished? If not, where would you draw the line? When is violence acceptable / excused in your (cultural, national, community) context?

Violence is something that needs to be recognised. In other words, when we think about violence, we are influenced by socially, culturally and politically constructed notions of violence for example good violence, bad violence and understandable violence. The following definitions suggest a variety of ways to think about violence:

- Physical violence "…involves acts carried out with knowledge of the likely consequences for the other person including pain and injury." [3]
- Violence is "…anything avoidable that hinders human self-realisation." as expressed by Johann Galtung
- "Violence is a means of control and oppression that can include emotional, social or economic force, coercion or pressure, as well as physical harm. It can be overt, in the form of physical assault or threatening someone with a weapon; it can also be overt, in the form of intimidation, threats, persecution deception or other forms of psychological or social pressure. The person targeted by this kind of violence is compelled to behave as expected or to act against her/his will out of fear." IRIN (UN Office for the Constitution of Humanitarian Affairs) [4]

Violence is an issue of responsibility towards others and ourselves. The issue of personal responsibility is crucial for effective prevention and intervention, particularly – and here we could look at our own reactions to any everyday act of violence, including gender-based – as there is a tendency to place some or even most of the responsibility on the victims of violence. 'Victim-blaming' exists to a certain degree with all forms of violence and is at least partially an obvious psychological reaction. In order not to question the safety of the world around us when we hear of a violent incident, we may examine the behaviour of the victim and assure ourselves that if we avoid such risks and behaviour (e.g. being out late alone, going into certain districts, leaving our door unlocked, dressing in a 'provocative' way) we will avoid violence. This natural act of psychological self-defence, however, focuses our attention on the perceived responsibility of the victim, and may neglect to fully question the conduct of the perpetrator.

Furthermore, there are many common ways in which gender-based violence is specifically excused, just as with any other occasion of violence, where an oppressive social structure is involved, and the violence is committed by somebody from the 'power-group' against somebody from the 'group with less power'. Many factors – difficult childhoods, psychological factors, or the perceived complicity of victims – are used to explain the occurrence of gender-based violence. Nevertheless, if preventing violence involves a responsibility to ourselves and others, it is important that these factors are not used in general social discussions to lessen the responsibility of perpetrators.

gender matters

> **Reflection**
> - Develop a list of the different forms of *gender-based violence* you know of in society. Try to list a concrete example for every form identified.
> - What are the most typical reactions that you have experienced regarding the different forms of violence and gender-based violence listed?
> - Do these reactions involve victim-blaming and forms of mitigation? Do other forms of interpersonal violence evoke similar reactions?

2.2.1 Aggression and violence

Is violence natural? Is violence an issue of sex or gender? Are violence and aggression the same? What is the relationship of these two words to each other in your language? Is a physical attack always considered as violence? Is there a difference in judging violence depending on the identity of the perpetrator and the victim?

The words 'aggression' and 'violence' are often used interchangeably, yet they do not mean the same thing. 'Aggression' is something we can experience in situations that are physically or emotionally threatening to us. The 'fight or flight' reactions that we experience in such situations have a biochemical background and are closely related to the self-preservation instinct of most species, including humans. In anger-management training courses and programmes for violent offenders, it is advised that it is possible to exercise control over our aggressive potential. In a matter of seconds we can assess whether it is 'appropriate' to use violence in a certain situation or not. In developing a gender perspective on violence, many practitioners argue that *violence is the decision to use one's aggressive potential to hurt another person's integrity.*

This definition is not the only possible way to look at violence, however. Manuela Martinez, who has researched violence and aggression in both humans and animals, points out that "it is very difficult to differentiate between aggression and violence in humans". She uses the word 'aggression' to refer to the behaviour of animals, "as in this case this behaviour has a very specific purpose (survival of the individual and the species) and it is, in general, very well controlled and ritualised". In the case of humans, however, she considers the same behaviour to be violence "…as there is no relation between the harm caused in the victim and the objective of the behaviour". [5]

As the example below suggests, there are tangible differences between a sudden aggressive action that is the result of an immediate threat to physical or mental integrity, and a violent action that results from the desire of (in this case male) privilege to 'punish' behaviour found to be unacceptable.

"Everybody envied me for my boyfriend. He was very popular at school, a charming and handsome young man, always polite with teachers, respectful to his and my parents. But sometimes, when we were on our own and I did something he did not like (like going out with the girls), he would shout at me. Later came the kicks and shoves. I could not tell anybody I knew because all my friends, my parents, and his parents were so impressed with what a nice a guy he was." (6)

If our aggressive potential is an evolutionary development, designed to aid self-preservation, then this impulse is present in everybody, whether male or female. As chapter one outlined, however, expressions and behaviours are gendered, and our societies demand very specific responses in certain situations. An aspect of the socialisation processes discussed in the previous chapter is that from early childhood boys and girls may come to feel that they are supposed to react differently to their anger or fear, feelings that typically trigger aggressive reactions. You can think about this again by examining again the discussions of masculinity in section 1.4. Apart from handling our aggressive potential according to our gender and gender experience, we also learn about other limiting factors, such as the age group we belong to. For example, corporal punishment of children and young people by parents or teachers is allowed in many legal systems either by the word or practice of the law, whereas a similar slap between adults is judged differently both by the courts and by the public.

Reflection

This short reflection works through perceptions of violence in our surroundings.

1. Think of several situations when you were angry with different people such as friends, teachers, parents, or a trainer. List the different ways in which you have reacted in each situation. Can you recognize certain patterns in the ways you have reacted to frustrating situations in the past?
2. Think of your grandparents and others of their generation and the treatment of violence in their time (if you know anything about it). Think of your parents and their attitudes to violence, and what is considered acceptable and unacceptable. Think of your own approach to violence today. Has this changed from one generation to the next?
3. Try to find out about the criminal statistics for violent crimes in your country. The Ministry of Justice, the central police headquarters, statistical office or attorney general's office are usually obliged to publish such data. As they all act in the name of citizens, these statistics are public data and should be freely accessible to everyone. Look for figures on murder, manslaughter, serious bodily injury, sexual crimes and also on crimes related to child neglect (parental neglect). Check whether the official statistics record the sex of offenders and victims. If they do, create a table showing how commonly men and women become victims or perpetrators of different crimes. Based on the previous discussions related to gender and socialisation, discuss whether participants can recognize connections between gender socialisation and criminal statistics.
4. Find out about the legal provisions in your country or countries for parents 'disciplining' their children with the use of violence. Is it different from what is allowed between strangers, whether adults, or an adult and a child?

2.2.2 Abuse and violent incidents

What constitutes abuse? Yesterday I shouted at my boyfriend/girlfriend: does that mean I'm abusive? I've done or experienced something from the lists of violence: am I an abuser, or am I being abused?

Abuse is something ongoing; therefore it requires some form of relationship between the abuser and the abused. This relationship can initially be wanted by both parties (as in the case of an intimate relationship), but it can be relationships initiated by one party only (child-parent relationship), or something that is a result of social factors (such as teacher-student or neighbours). Just as with differentiating between 'violence' and 'aggression', separating 'violent incidents' and 'abuse' can be challenging. Some of the differences between 'violent incident' and 'abuse' can be highlighted as follows:

Violent incident in a relationship
- occasional and irregular
- both parties can initiate
- it can be discussed between the parties; the discussion changes the behaviour of the person who caused the conflict
- as the partners know more and more about each other, conflict probably lessens
- the instigator-causer of the conflict feels responsible
- it is an issue of two people who take into account the views of both
- spontaneous, often a reaction to outside factors (frustration, tiredness, being afraid of something)
- what was done can be compensated for
- solution is within the relationship

Abusive relationship
- regular incidents
- the roles are always the same
- it escalates: a series of more and more serious one-sided conflicts
- it cannot be discussed successfully; there are no changes after discussion
- the perpetrator often prepares consciously
- the perpetrator does not take responsibility, and holds victim responsible
- one-dimensional issue: acknowledges the views of only one
- what was done cannot (should not) be excused
- the abuse is done with the support of power imbalances (gender roles, physical power, economic influence)
- the feelings of the victim: helplessness, fear, self-blame
- solution can only come through outside means (divorce, police intervention, separate therapy / self-help)

These lists contain probabilities, and for a relationship to be seen as abusive - rather than just containing violent incidents - typically several items on the list have to be relevant. Some actions present on the 'abuse list' hurt the psychological and physical integrity of the other to such an extent that even one instance entails abuse. As a general guide, abuse is an ongoing and imbalanced system of oppression, committed by groups or individuals against groups or individuals.

Measuring abuse and violent incidents in society...

When an ongoing violent relationship and individual incidents of aggression are both counted as violence, it is very easy to come to the false conclusion that women and men experience similar levels of violence in intimate relationships. This can be seen, for example, in an article published in *The Guardian* [7]: the article gives an overview of the findings of the 1999 UK Home Office Research Study on domestic violence [8], which stated - on the basis of a self-completion questionnaire included in the British Crime Survey - that the percentage of male and female population to have experienced any type of physical assault from a partner or former partner in the previous year was the same (4.2%). Just one paragraph later, the research summary mentions that 'women were more likely to have been assaulted three or more times'. However, the title of the article reads: 'Both sexes equally likely to suffer domestic violence', thereby equating one-time physical assaults of any type with the ongoing process of domestic violence.

This headline equates one-off violent incidents with ongoing abuse, and does not give information on the power and psycho-social relations. A later Home Office research study by Sylvia Walby and Jonathan Allen [9] for example, pointed out that it was more typical for men to have experienced only one incidence of violence, whereas it was more typical for women to experience repeated acts of violence by the same person, 'with women constituting 89% of all those who suffered four or more incidents'. As Myra Marx Ferre, a U.S. researcher put it when discussing studies on violence against women and men, "[t]he ability to discern and analyse the differences between simple acts of violence and patterns of domestic terrorism are crucial". [10]

2.2.3 Violence in the public and private sphere

Does the government have a say in something that happens in the home? Do men / women experience violence in the same way?

The ethical, moral and legal frameworks of the Council of Europe member countries have historically been concerned with violence as something existing in the public sphere, whereas the private (domestic) sphere was idealised as a space apart from society, ideally untouched by society's influence. Civil and political rights (the so-called first-generation rights)[4], for example, are mainly concerned with violence in the public sphere and with limiting the state and its representatives in perpetrating violence as a means to abuse power. This has meant that specific forms of violence against women have gone unnoticed, or have only been gradually addressed. For a long time in history, the inferior position of women or certain ethnic or racial minorities was considered natural. Therefore acts that are now considered human rights violations were not widely condemned because the victims of these violations were not acknowledged by those in power in society to have those rights.

---

4 A short explanation of the three generations of human rights can be found in COMPASS, the manual on human rights education with young people, Council of Europe, 2002 under the sub-heading "The evolution of human rights" at www.coe.int/compass.

gender matters

Although reliable, gender-sensitive statistics are still rare in most Council of Europe member countries, there is evidence to suggest that women and men experience violence in different ways[5]. The World Health Organisation's *World Report on Violence and Health* notes that whereas men '…are much more likely to be attacked by a stranger or an acquaintance than by someone within their close circle of relationships…one of the most common forms of violence against women is that performed by a husband or male partner' [11]. In other words, women experience more violence in the private sphere, whereas for men it is more likely to occur in the public sphere.

An extreme case in point is the issue of rape in war: it has only recently been 'recognised' as a war crime, despite the fact that the concept of war crimes has existed since the Second World War (and mass rape was perpetrated throughout that conflict). The Balkan wars of the first half of the 1990s marked a turning point: pressure from women's rights activists and media coverage resulted in rape being included in the list of war crimes[6]. A European Community fact-finding team estimates that more than 20,000 Muslim women were raped during the war in Bosnia [12].

It is important, however, not to approach gender-based violence in conflict situations as something separate or different. Some women's organisations in the Balkan region organised themselves primarily to support women victims of war, only to find out that the 'war on women' was there in peacetime as well: "Violence against women in wartime is a reflection of violence against women in peacetime, as long as violence against women is pervasive and accepted; stress, small arms proliferation and a culture of violence push violence against women to epidemic proportions, especially when civilians are the main targets of warfare." [13]

Similarly, recognising the forms of violence that lesbian women, gay men, bisexuals and transgendered people face is a recent and slow process. This is hardly surprising given that LGBT issues are still marginalised in many countries, and LGBT often lack explicit representation in structures and institutions that frame human realities and our responses to issues. Including violence against LGBT has been influential in moving to an understanding of gender-based violence

---

5 "The production of gender statistics requires not only that all official data are collected by sex, but also that concepts and methods used in data collection and presentation adequately reflect gender issues in society and take in consideration all factors that can produce gender-based bias." Source: http://www.ilo.org/public/english/region/asro/mdtmanila/training/unit3/infgsens.htm

6 "Rape was specifically identified as a war crime for the first time in the Tokyo War Crimes Trials after World War II, when commanders were held responsible for rapes committed by soldiers under their command. In January 1993, the UN sent a medical team to investigate rape in the former Yugoslavia. In light of evidence of rape perpetrated on a massive scale, the UN Commission on Human Rights passed a resolution placing rape, for the first time, clearly within the framework of war crimes and called for an international tribunal to prosecute these crimes." Source: http://www.phrusa.org/research/health_effects/humrape.html#d
In December 1998 the International Criminal Tribunal for the former Yugoslavia (ICTY) passed a judgment which determined the elements of rape under international law (Prosecutor v. Furundzija, ICTY press release: http://www.un.org/icty/pressreal/p372-e.htm). In February 2001 the tribunal delivered a ruling that made mass systematic rape and sexual enslavement in a time of war a crime against humanity. (Prosecutor v. Kunarac and others, ICTY press release: Source: http://www.un.org/icty/pressreal/p566-e.htm)

that is broader than a sex-based definition of violence against women. Gender-based violence *against* LGBT individuals is usually known as 'gay bashing', which is the physical, psychological or verbal assault of a lesbian or homosexual on account of his or her sexual orientation.

2.3 Types of violence

Is violence only physical? What forms can violence take? Are all forms of violence criminalized?

We are used to associating violence predominantly with physical violence. According to The American Heritage Dictionary of the English Language, *for example, violence is* 'physical force exerted for the purpose of violating, damaging, or abusing'. To understand gender-based violence, however, we need to broaden our associations. As Johann Galtung defined, violence can be seen as anything avoidable that obstructs human self-realisation. Victims of verbal attack, of sexual violence, of systematic economic deprivation by a partner or of threatening behaviour would identify themselves also as victims of violence.

Violence is a difficult and complex issue, and categorising different 'types' of violence can never be exact. For discussion purposes, however, it is useful to start with a framework for discussion (which may also prove useful during group work). In this publication we will distinguish five inter-related types of violence: physical, verbal, sexual(ised), psychological and socio-economic. In reality, some or many forms can be present at the same time, particularly in abusive relationships. All forms can occur both in the private sphere (in families and intimate relationships) and in the public sphere, committed by unknown individuals in public space, or by organisations, institutions, and states. It is also important to stress that although some forms of gender-based violence are considered to be typical for (married) couples and generally adults, studies and experience show that young women and men are similarly affected[7].

a) Physical violence

Physical violence includes beating, burning, kicking, punching, biting, maiming or killing, the use of objects or weapons, or tearing out one's hair. Some classifications also include trafficking and slavery in the category of physical violence because initial coercion is often experienced, and the young women and men involved end up becoming victims of further violence as a result of their enslavement.

---

7   For example the US website www.coolnurse.com notes: 'In 1995, 7 percent of all murder victims were young women who were killed by their boyfriends. One in five or 20 percent of dating couples report some type of violence in their relationship. One in five college females will experience some form of dating violence. A survey of 500 young women aged 15 to 24 found that 60 percent were currently involved in an ongoing abusive relationship and all participants had experienced violence in a dating relationship. One study found that 38 percent of date rape victims were young women from 14 to 17 years of age. ... More than 4 in every 10 incidents of domestic violence involve non-married persons. (Bureau of Justice Special Report: Intimate Partner Violence, May 2001, other statistic from the U.S. Department of Justice)

Physical violence in the private sphere

Physical violence is an act attempting to or resulting in pain and / or physical injury. As with all forms of violence, the main aim of the perpetrator is not only - or may not always be - to cause physical pain, but to limit the other's self-determination. Physical violence sends a clear message to the victim from the perpetrator: "I can do things to you that you do not want to happen." Such violence demonstrates differences of social power, or may intend to promote particular demands through coercion. Gender-based violence in intimate relationships, often referred to as domestic violence, continues to be a distressing phenomenon in every country. According to the Council of Europe, domestic violence is the major cause of death and disability for women aged 16 to 44 and accounts for more death and ill-health than cancer or traffic accidents [14]. Amnesty International quotes a Russian government estimate which states that '14,000 women were killed by their partners or relatives in 1999' [15].

Physical violence in the private sphere affects young people to a great degree. Both common sense and international studies show that witnessing the abuse of one parent by another results in serious psychological harm to children. Often, children and young people present during an act of spousal abuse will also be injured, sometimes by accident and sometimes because they try to intervene. Young men often commit criminal offences against the abusive parent (mostly fathers) in order to protect their mothers and siblings. Children regularly become the victims of a revenge of the abuser on the mother. In fact, for many mothers a prime motivation to stay in an abusive relationship is that the abuser threatens to harm or kill the children if she tries to leave.

> *"No one thinks enough of the kids – or thinks what effect it has on them. It doesn't just affect the mother – it's the kids ... because they're the ones that have got to see it and hear it." (17-year-old girl)* [16]

Physical violence also appears in the intimate relationships of young people: couples do not necessarily have to share accommodation or have children for physical violence in the relationship to take place. Because of this assumption, however, young people may feel there is a difficulty in talking about it. As the above quoted Council of Europe data shows, women as young as 16 die regularly as a result of domestic violence; dating relationships can even end with the death of the abused when the victim is in their early teens[8].

Physical violence in the public sphere

Gender-based violence in public is often related to assumptions and expectations concerning gender-roles. Verbal abuse, name-calling, threats and attacks may take place, and

---

8 NANE Women's Rights Association observed homicides related to intimate partner violence as reported in the newspapers in two consecutive years. Between September 2002 and September 2004 there were 13 underage victims of intimate partnership violence between the ages of 2 months and 17 years. In some cases their death was a way to take revenge on the partner trying to escape an abusive relationship; in other cases the perpetrator accidentally killed the child.

it is common that LGBTs or those perceived to be gay, lesbian or 'different' may become victims of public violence. Violence against LGBTs can be organised (groups going to well known meeting places of gay men to beat them up) or 'spontaneous' outbursts of violence, for example, when a lesbian woman is attacked when she walks on the street and holds hands with her partner in public. In this respect it is a safety issue, and research shows that many LGBTs refrain from showing affection in public for fear of being beaten up. This kind of street violence usually remains underreported.

> A.-L.H. and three of his friends were attacked on Sunday 11th July, 2004 around 3:30am, returning from a gay party which took place in Belgrade. They came out of the club and were suddenly attacked from behind by at least four hooligans about a hundred metres from the club entrance. The hooligans were hitting them with bats and clubs shouting, "You want a party, Fags? Well here's a party for you!" They attacked all of them; some were kicking while at least two of them were hitting him with bats. His left forearm was badly cut with an unidentified sharp object. The attackers gave L. the following severe body injuries: a broken tooth and nose, a cut of 7-8 cm long on his left forearm, a cut on his lower lip and swellings under his eyes. [17]

b) Verbal violence

Many cultures have sayings or expressions that state that words are harmless: there is a long tradition that teaches us to ignore verbal attacks. However, when these attacks become regular and systematic and purposefully target our sensitive spots[9], the object of these attacks is right to consider themselves subjected to verbal abuse.

Verbal violence in the private sphere

Contrary to a functional relationship in which partners recognise each other's sensitive areas in time and take special care not to hurt each other in those areas, one who is verbally abusive will especially aim at hurting with words and tones.

Verbal abuse can include issues that are *person-related*, such as put-downs (in private or in front of others), ridiculing, the use of swear-words that are especially uncomfortable for the other, saying bad things about the loved ones of the other (family, friends), threatening with other forms of violence against the victim or against somebody or something dear to them. Other times the verbal abuse is *related to the background* of the victim, such as religion, culture, language, (perceived) sexual orientation or traditions. Depending on the most emotionally sensitive areas of the victim, abusers consciously target these issues in a way that is painful, humiliating and threatening to the victim.

---

9   'Sensitive spots' can be anything that one is especially emotional about. It can be an important person, one's religion or ethnic identity. It can be also something that one is ashamed of (whether it is justified or not, whether it is the product of internalised oppression or personal conviction).

Verbal violence in the public sphere

Most of the verbal violence that women experience because of being women is sexualised, and is listed under sexual violence. Once more, verbal GBV in the public sphere is largely related to gender-roles: they include comments and jokes about the 'stupidity' of women or they present women as sex objects (jokes about sexual availability, prostitution, rape). A large amount of bullying is related to the (perceived) sexuality of young people (especially boys). The regular negative use of words such as 'queer' or 'fag' is often traumatising for those perceived as gays and lesbians. This is very likely one of the reasons why many gays and lesbians only 'come out' after secondary school.

c) Psychological violence

All forms of violence have a psychological aspect, since the main aim of being violent or abusive is to hurt the integrity and dignity of another person. Apart from this, there are some forms of violence which are communicated through conducts that cannot be placed in the other categories, and therefore can be said to achieve psychological violence in a 'pure' form. This can include isolation or confinement, withholding information, disinformation, and threatening behaviour.

Psychological violence in the private sphere

Psychological violence can be, for example, threatening conducts which lack physical violence or verbal elements. They can be actions that refer to former acts of violence, or purposeful ignorance and neglect of the other.

Psychological violence in the public sphere

A common form includes the isolation of young women or men who do not act according to gender roles. Isolation in the public sphere is most often used by peer groups, but responsible adults, such as teachers and sports coaches, can also be perpetrators. Most typically it means exclusion from certain group activities. It can also include intimidation in a similar fashion to psychological abuse in the private sphere.

d) Sexual(ised) violence

The term 'sexual*ised*' is increasingly used to stress an important aspect of this type of violence, namely that of using sexuality as a terrain for attack is merely another tool to inflict damage, rather than anything related to the sexuality of either perpetrator or victim. Sexual violence has often been related to the behaviour of the victim (explicit sexual behaviour or dressing in the public sphere, denial of sexual availability in the private sphere) or related to the sexual needs of the perpetrator (sexual frustration). This is called 'relativisation', and is one of the methods through which different players in society try to ignore the seriousness of gender-based violence. Relativisation means that the criminal act of rape, for example, is not judged as an act on its own, but relative to the perceived behaviour of the victim. It may also include misguided attempts to consider factors on the perpetrators' side which make their action 'understandable'.

As more and more data has become available on the true circumstances of sexual violence related to both victims and perpetrators, it has become clear that sexual(ised) violence, as with every other form of violence, is related to the power structure between abuser(s) and abused. Sexual(ised) violence includes many actions that are equally hurtful to every victim and are used similarly in the public and private sphere; examples include rape (sexual violence including some form of penetration of the victim's body), marital rape and attempted rape. Other types of forced sexual activities include being forced to watch somebody masturbate, forcing somebody to masturbate in front of others, forced unsafe sex, sexual harassment, and, in the case of women, abuse related to reproduction (forced pregnancy, forced abortion, forced sterilisation).

Sexualised violence in the private sphere

Some forms of sexual(ised) violence, which are related to the particular victim's personal limits, are more typical of the private sphere: the perpetrator violates these limits on purpose, such as date rape, forcing certain types of sexual activities, withdrawal of sexual attention as a tool of punishment, forcing the other(s) to watch (and sometimes to imitate) pornography.

Sexualised violence in the public sphere

The different forms of sexual(ised) violence appear without exception in both the private and the public sphere. There are however three forms of sexual violence in the public sphere which need to be noted because of their impact on victims and potential victims: sexual harassment at the workplace, sexual violence as a weapon of war and torture, and sexual violence against (perceived) LGBT as a means of 'punishment' for abandoning prescribed gender-roles.

> **Definition:**
> **Rape**: The invasion of any part of the body of the victim or of the perpetrator with a sexual organ, or of the anal or genital opening of the victim with any object or any other part of the body by force, coercion, taking advantage of a coercive environment, or against a person incapable of giving genuine consent (International Criminal Court)
> **Sexual exploitation**: Any abuse of position of vulnerability, differential power, or trust for sexual purposes; this includes profiting momentarily, socially, or politically from the sexual exploitation of another (United Nations Inter Agency Standing Committee)
> **Sexual harassment**: Any unwelcome, usually repeated and unreciprocated sexual advance, unsolicited sexual attention, demand for sexual access or favours, sexual innuendo or other verbal or physical conduct of a sexual nature, display of pornographic material, when it interferes with work, is made a condition of employment or creates an intimidating, hostile or offensive work environment (United Nations High Commission for Refugees)
> **Date rape**: a rape that is committed by the person with whom the victim is on a date. The term originated in the 1980s, when the phenomenon became widely discussed.

> **Reflection**
>
> Consider the definitions offered in the box above.
> What are the relevant definitions in the criminal code of your country? Are there differences? Which definition do you prefer? Why?
> In what context do these issues come up in your/a group of young people?

e) Socio-economic violence

This form of violence can be both a means to make the victim more vulnerable to other forms of violence, but can also be the reason why other forms of violence are inflicted. Whereas world economic figures clearly show that one of the results of neo-liberal globalisation is the feminisation of poverty[10] (making women generally more economically vulnerable than men), economic vulnerability is a phenomenon that exists on a personal level as well. It has been recognised in a vast number of abusive relationships as a distinct phenomenon, and that is why it has merited a category of its own. At the same time, a woman's better economic status in a relationship does not necessarily eliminate the threat of violence because this can also lead to conflicts about status and emasculation in abusive relationships.

Socio-economic violence in the private sphere

Most typical forms of socio-economic violence include taking away the earnings of the victim, not allowing them to have a separate income ('housewife' status, working in the family business without a salary), or making her or him unfit for work through targeted physical abuse.

> *"We got married right after high-school, and I got pregnant at 19. I stayed at home for the next three years on maternity leave. He started to beat me regularly after our child was born, but he always took great care to hit me on places where it would not show: on my torso or where my head was covered with hair, so that our friends and family would not see it and ask questions. I would not have said anything to anyone because we are a middle-class family, and nobody would have believed that things like this happen outside poor ethnic families. After the three years were over, I wanted to study and get a part-time job. That was when he also started to beat my face. I missed my oral entry exam, and I started to miss whole weeks from work because I*

---

10 According to the Beijing Platform for Action, '[m]ore than 1 billion people in the world today, the great majority of whom are women, live in unacceptable conditions of poverty.' (Adopted at the Fourth World Conference on Women, 1995)
'Millions of women in developing countries live in poverty. The feminization of poverty is a growing phenomenon. Women are still the poorest of the world's poor, representing 70 percent of the 1.3 billion people who live in absolute poverty. When nearly 900 million women have incomes of less than $1 a day, the association between gender inequality and poverty remains a harrowing reality.' UNIFEM, Strengthening Women's Economic Capacity
'Women work two-thirds of the world's working hours, produce half of the world's food, and yet earn only 10% of the world's income and own less than 1% of the world's property.' World Development Indicators, 1997, Womankind Worldwide

could not have gone to work with black eyes, or a swollen nose. It would have been so shameful! Eventually I was fired, as the company could not afford to have an employee missing work week after week with no plausible explanation." [18]

Socio-economic violence in the public sphere

Socio-economic violence in the public sphere is both a cause and an effect of dominant gender power relations in societies. It can include denial of access to education or (equally) paid work (mainly to women), the denial of access to services, exclusion from certain jobs, the denial of the enjoyment and exercise of civil, cultural, social, political rights, and, as is sometimes the case for LGBTs, results in criminalisation.

Some public forms of socio-economic gender-based violence contribute to women becoming economically dependent on their partner (lower wages, very low or no child-care benefits, or benefits tied to the income tax of the wage-earning male partner). This in return gives a person with a tendency to be abusive in his relationships the chance to act without any fear of losing his partner.

> **Reflection**
>
> Who are the most vulnerable groups to socio-economic violence in your environment?
> In your experience does the state inflict this kind of violence?

2.4 Gender-based violence in a human rights framework

Is there a need for a special convention on women's rights? What does the UN term 'harmful traditional practices' mean? How do we distinguish between cultural respect and cultural relativism, and who should decide about it?

In our contemporary world *human rights conventions and declarations* have become important symbolic and legal instruments for a variety of issues. This is a relatively new development; a widespread acknowledgement of human rights was basically absent from international relations until the Second World War; however, the Shoah (Holocaust) served as the catalyst "…that made human rights an issue in world politics".[19].

One of the most important international human rights documents dealing with women's rights is the United Nations 'Convention on the Elimination of All Forms of Discrimination Against Women' (CEDAW) [20]. This Convention prohibits discrimination on the basis of sex. It defines discrimination against women as:

> *Any distinction, exclusion or restriction made on the basis of sex which has the effect or purpose of impairing or nullifying the recognition, enjoyment or exercise by women, irrespective of their marital status, on a basis of equality of men and women, of human rights and fundamental freedoms in the political, social, cultural, civil or any other field.* [21]

States that are parties to the Convention are obliged to adopt all necessary measures to ensure that women enjoy equality with men, meaning that they should adopt necessary legislation combating discrimination and advancing women's rights. This, however, does not mean that women can be denied special protection by a state in relation to maternity.

CEDAW reviews compliance by states with the Convention. States have to submit periodic reports on the measures undertaken to implement the Convention. The CEDAW Committee monitors states' compliance; however, its implementation mechanism is regarded as weak, and it relies on the force of moral persuasion. Another flaw is that there are many reservations and exceptions negotiated by states that have been added to this document[11].

Reflection

Where does your country stand?
Find out whether your country has ratified the convention, and, if it has, whether there are any official reservations relating to the CEDAW convention. www.un.org/womenwatch/daw/cedaw/reservations-country.htm

Violence against women – unlike other issues such as suffrage (the right to vote), equality, or discrimination – is a more recent focus of international human rights agendas. CEDAW, which dates back to 1979 and came into force in 1981, mentions 'discrimination' twenty-two times, 'equal' or 'equality' thirty-four times, 'human rights' five times, but makes no mention of violence, rape, abuse or battery [22]. However, in 1992 General Recommendation 19 was issued by the CEDAW Committee, recommending that violence against women should also be reported on by the state parties. The CEDAW Convention has recently added an individual complaint mechanism, whereby individuals, after exhausting domestic remedies, can file a complaint as to the State's compliance with provisions of the Convention.

In 1993 in Vienna the United Nations General Assembly adopted the 'Declaration on the Elimination of Violence Against Women', where violence was defined as

> *Any act of gender-based violence that results in, or is likely to result in, physical, sexual or psychological harm or suffering to women, including threats of such acts, coercion or arbitrary deprivation of liberty, whether occurring in public or in private life.* [23]

This Declaration was significant in that it made violence against women an international

---

[11] 'Article 28, paragraph 2, of the Convention adopts the impermissibility principle contained in the Vienna Convention on the Law of Treaties. It states that a reservation incompatible with the object and purpose of the present Convention shall not be permitted. The Committee in two of the general recommendations and its statement on reservations has called on the States to re-examine their self-imposed limitations to full compliance with all the principles in the Convention by the entry of reservations. Removal or modification of reservations, particularly to articles 2 and 16, would indicate a State party's determination to remove all barriers to women's full equality and its commitment to ensuring that women are able to participate fully in all aspects of public and private life without fear of discrimination or recrimination. States which remove reservations would be making a major contribution to achieving the objectives of both formal and de facto or substantive compliance with the Convention.' Source: http://www.un.org/womenwatch/daw/cedaw/reservations.htm

issue, and not subject to arguments about cultural relativism. There are many ways of understanding and discussing cultural relativism, but in the post-World War Two international arena it developed as a way of countering racist and fascist ideologies of cultural, racial or civilisational superiority. Influential anthropologists such as Claude Lévi-Strauss, and institutions such as UNESCO argued that "…racism could be overcome by recognising the problem of ethnocentrism, by promoting the benefits of cultural diversity in enriching society and by encouraging greater knowledge of other cultures among western societies" [24]. While understandable in this context, the belief that racism and oppression can be eradicated through greater knowledge and tolerance has encountered many problems. This is especially the case when cultural difference is used to explain or justify the human rights abuse of women. Therefore, this Declaration included a variety of what have been termed *harmful traditional practices* such as female genital mutilation, rape and torture, domestic battery and female sexual slavery. This was an important statement from the UN and it placed individual rights to physical integrity above cultural rights. It also recognised that national or cultural support for such practices are not representative of the wishes of women, and that, indeed, many voices in supposedly homogenous cultures are also opposed to these practices.

Another aspect of the Declaration is that it recognises the need to rethink apparently common sense boundaries between public and private, a challenge long advocated by feminist groups. The UN Declaration prohibits both state violence against women and private violence, including '…battering, sexual abuse of female children in the household, dowry-related violence, marital rape, female genital mutilation and other traditional practices harmful to women, non-spousal violence or violence related to exploitation' [25]. The Declaration also prohibits violence against women based on cultural practices. Although it is not a binding document, the Declaration contributed to breaking the wall of silence and recognising violence against women as an international human rights violation.

The 'European Convention on Human Rights' does not have special provisions relating to women's rights or gender-based violence. It does stipulate, however, that private and family life should be protected (Article 8), men and women of marriageable age should have the right to marriage (Article 12) and that spouses should have equal rights in marriage (Article 5, Protocol 7). The Convention has a strong and well-known enforcement mechanism, the European Court of Human Rights (ECHR), which receives individual as well as state vs. state complaints.

Reflection

Visit the HUDOC database on the European Court of Human Rights website and find out about judgements and dismissed cases related to gender-based violence involving your country / state.
http://www.echr.coe.int/echr

Violence against women is no longer a private issue: it has been recognized as a human rights violation, and as a violation of an individual's psychological and physical integrity. Yet recognition and legal measures are not enough. Violence prevention is a priority, and effective mechanisms and processes for violence prevention and gender mainstreaming also need to be in place. Apart from the international human rights bodies already discussed, other important mechanisms are:

- National committees for gender advancement with a clear plan of action
- An equality Ombudsman
- Effective legislation implemented to ensure legal and substantive equality
- Quotas for women in education and employment (for example, affirmative action measures)
- In civil society, women's NGOs and women's studies in universities have important critical and lobbying roles

2.5 Gender-based violence against LGBT

Is violence against LGBT gender-based violence? What examples can you think of to explain your answer?

Violence against lesbians, gays, bisexuals and transgenders (LGBT) is often neglected when gender-based violence is discussed. However, as we have seen in 1.3.4, gender and sexuality are two closely interconnected concepts. It is not unusual, for example, for perpetrators of violence against LGBTs to 'justify' their actions through expressing disgust at gay sexuality or gay masculinities. This neglect of gender-based violence against LGBTs partly reflects the lack of information we have, and the lack of legal and other forms of protection for LGBT in many countries in Europe and the rest of the world. There is no universal legal document that deals with or protects sexual minorities; LGBTs face "… continued exclusion from the full protection of international human rights norms" **(26)**. The recent inability of the UN Human Rights Commission to adopt a document that would explicitly recognize homosexuals highlights how LGBTs suffer from an unequal situation in comparison to heterosexual citizens[12].

2.6 Domestic violence and violence in intimate relationships

What is the content of current public discourse in your country in relation to domestic violence? What are the human rights arguments most often quoted in relation to domestic violence?

Domestic violence, or intimate partnership violence, is the most common type of gender-based violence. It also requires special consideration because it is a relational type of

---

12 Brazil introduced a draft resolution entitled, 'Human Rights and Sexual Orientation', which addresses the topic of equal rights for gays and lesbians. It called, among others, "upon all States to promote and protect the human rights of all persons regardless of their sexual orientation".

violence, and the dynamics are therefore very different from violent incidents that occur among strangers.

Considering domestic violence as a private, domestic issue has significantly hampered recognition of the phenomenon as a human rights violation. The invisibility of the phenomenon was exacerbated by the fact that traditionally, international human rights law was believed to be applicable to relations between individual and the state (or the states), and human rights organisations focused only on politically motivated violations (such as torture or the inhumane treatment of prisoners). However, it has gradually become recognised that state responsibility under international law can arise not only from state action, but also from state inaction where the state fails to protect its citizens from violent crimes.

> **Definition:**
> Domestic violence includes "forms of violence that perpetuate and exploit the dichotomy between women and men in order to assure the subordination and inferiority of women and everything associated with the feminine". Although domestic violence occurs in same sex relationships just as often as in heterosexual relationships (1 in 4), and there are cases of women abusing their male partners, the vast majority of domestic violence is perpetrated against women by men.
> Domestic violence (rape, battering, sexual or psychological abuse) leads to severe physical and mental suffering, injuries and often death. It is inflicted against the will of the person, with the purpose being to humiliate, intimidate and control the victim, and very often the victim is left without recourse to any remedies: the police and law enforcement mechanisms are often gender-insensitive, hostile or absent. [27]

A question often asked in relation to domestic violence is 'why doesn't (s)he leave?' There is no simple answer because domestic violence is a complex phenomenon which involves physical, psychological, emotional and economic forms of abuse. It may often cause 'battered woman syndrome', where a woman in an abusive relationship starts feeling helpless, worthless, powerless and accepting of the status quo. Yet this term fails to explain many things, including why some women kill their violent partners, and other reasons why women stay in a violent relationship. These reasons include financial dependence on the abuser, social constraints, and a lack of alternatives such as shelters for abuse victims. Domestic violence often involves isolation of the victim from the family and friends, deprivation of personal possessions, manipulation of children, threats of reprisals against her and her children or other family members. Furthermore, common social pressures regarding the nature of the family – 'some kind of father is better than no father for your children' - makes getting out of an abusive relationship not only difficult but also extremely dangerous.

A further reason is the much-documented phenomenon of the 'Cycle of Violence'.

The abusive behaviour involved in this cycle is sometimes instinctive and sometimes deliberate, and aims to keep the abused person in the relationship through promises and denials.

The basic cycle consists of an outburst of violence, which is followed by a so-called 'honeymoon period' characterised by a sudden positive change in the behaviour of the abuser. It is known as the honeymoon period because victims often describe this period as being very similar to the early part of the relationship. The abuser is typically very apologetic because of the violence inflicted, promises to change, and may even offer presents. However, this period does not last long as its only function is to eliminate the worries of the victim regarding the future of the relationship. The victim her or himself is typically party to this as nobody likes to remember negative experiences, and therefore the victim welcomes the apparent changes and promises made.

Once the victim's worries have been silenced, the old power structure is re-asserted. The many typical characteristics of domestic violence will again breed the kind of tension that eventually erupts in a further act of violence on the part of the abuser. Early in the relationship the violent incidents can be as far apart as six months or even a year, thereby making it difficult to recognise the cyclical nature. Early incidents are likely to be verbal incidents followed by minor acts of physical violence, which also make it hard for the victim to recognise that the put-downs, the breaking of cups, the shoves, the slaps and finally the beatings are parts of an escalating cycle.

The cycle not only escalates as far as the severity of violence is concerned, but the incidents typically become closer to each other. Eventually the honeymoon phase can completely disappear; in approximately 20% of abusive relationships it does not exist at all. It may be replaced, particularly in social groups where domestic violence and rigid gender roles are less accepted, by minimising or denial.

> *"The day after he hit me, I showed my boyfriend the marks on my arm and face. He looked at me and asked me what I had done to myself. I tried to explain to him that he had done this to me, to which he said, 'If I had hit you, you'd be dead.'"* [28]

In contexts where rigid gender roles are more determining, the batterer has more freedom to deny responsibility. The set of gender roles that we are taught to belong to as women and men contain many contradictions, or demands that cannot be fulfilled. At the same time, part of the hegemonic male gender role is to oversee women and children in fulfilling their roles, and if necessary, discipline them. These two conditions combine to create a common justification for those who are abusive in relationships because they can easily find something or another to (a) blame the woman for the violence committed against her, and (b) to claim the right to inflict it.

Rape is a serious crime in most national criminal codes. However, when it relates to family and intimate relationships, the situation becomes more complicated. Rape by those who were known and trusted by the victim can have more serious and long-lasting consequences than rape by a stranger. Nevertheless, rape in an intimate relationship is very difficult to prove: in domestic courts the defence of consent, the prior relationship of the victim and the perpetrator and the prior sexual conduct of the victim often make the experience of victims resorting to legal action humiliating and traumatising[13].

Domestic violence is cyclical

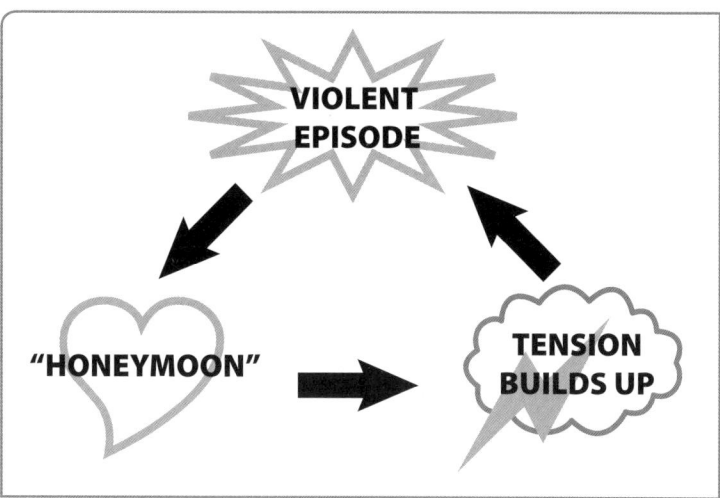

Physical abuse and emotional abuse, often accompanied by acts of sexual violence, have been perceived in many countries as acts or crimes of 'passion', motivated by jealousy or the failure of the partner to fulfil expectations. The influence of alcohol is also often cited as a mitigating factor. This ignores the fact that abuse is perpetrated in a systematic way. As Ronda Copelon remarks, alcohol does cause violence, but "many men get drunk without beating their wives and…men often beat their wives without being drunk. To the extent that alcohol facilitates male violence, it is an important factor in the effort to reduce violence, but it is not the cause" (29).

2.6.1 Domestic violence in LGBT relationships

Domestic violence in LGBT relationships is harder to identify, both for the victims and for the services offering support, because 'mainstream' services for domestic violence do not always recognise domestic violence in same sex relationships and are rarely experienced in dealing with its specific aspects. However, statistics show that violence in heterosexual, gay, and lesbian relationships occurs at approximately the same rate (one in four).

The main differences and similarities between same-gender and opposite-gender domestic violence are summarised below (30).

Similarities include the *form of abuse, the control* the perpetrator has over the victim, the *isolation* the abused may experience and the dynamics of the *'cycle of violence'*.

---

13 For the analysis of the issues of consent and coercion, see MacKinnon, C. 'Rape: on Coercion and Consent', in Weisberg, K. (Ed.). (1996). Sex, Violence, Work and Reproduction. Applications of Feminist Legal Theory to Women's Lives. Philadelphia: Temple University Press. (pp. 471-484).

Differences include:

Isolation: The isolation that accompanies domestic violence can be compounded by being LGBT in a homophobic society. Silence about domestic violence within the LGBT community further isolates the victim, giving more power to the batterer. Added to this is the problem of limited community space within LGBT networks: privacy may be difficult to maintain, and leaving made more difficult.

Heterosexist manipulation: A batterer may threaten to 'speak out about' a person's sexual orientation or gender identity to friends, family, co-workers, or a landlord. In addition to this, existing services may require an individual to 'come out' against his or her will.

Fear of further oppression: As an oppressed and defamed group, the LGBT community is often hesitant to address issues that many fear will further 'stain' the community.

Gender-based denial: The battered women's movement often avoids the fact that women do batter, and men are victims. This denial is also present among many police, hospital workers, and people in the criminal justice system.

Gender myths: People assume that two men in a fight must be equals. Similarly, Gay, bisexual and transgendered (GBT) men often reject the idea that they can be victims. It may also be assumed, given social assumptions about 'deviance', that this violence is part of a sadomasochistic one.

Context of historical oppression: LGBT people often approach shelters, social service agencies, domestic violence service-providers, police, and the courts with great caution. LGBT victims may fear re-victimization through homophobia, disbelief, rejection and degradation from institutions that have a history of exclusion, hostility and violence toward LGBT people.

> *"I had never been exposed to domestic violence through either experience or education. I am sure I was aware of it abstractly through the media but I never made the logical progression to realize that I, as a gay man, could be a victim. By not recognizing the abuse as domestic violence I never thought to reach out for help"* [31].

The organisation FORGE[14] writes that 'due to the fact that most Domestic Violence shelters and services are constructed around heterosexual women victims, gay (and straight) men who are battered or abused by women or men have no place in many organised systems for helping victims. Often, male victims are told that the only shelter options available to them are emergency housing for homeless people'.

---

14 www.forge-forward.org

Examples of good practice (where same sex couples are included in the work):

In Amsterdam a special 'hotline' for victims *and* perpetrators of domestic violence was recently launched. In an interview with two of the hotline volunteers, the volunteer used the more neutral term 'partner' and gave an example of domestic violence where a same sex couple was involved.

A survivor sharing her encounter with a poster on a university campus: "The first time I saw the poster about violence in gay and lesbian relationships, I just walked by thinking it had nothing to do with my life. On my way to lunch that afternoon, a few of the examples of abuse on it caught my eye. Over the next week I spent more and more time studying the poster. I realized that I was the target of these same behaviors in my relationship with Edie. That's how I ended up deciding to come to a support group." [32]

Endnotes for Chapter 2

(1) Source: http://wwww.reliefweb.int/w/rwb.nsf/s/40B847015485B34749256BFE0006E603)
(2) MacKinnon, C.A. (1987). *Feminism Unmodified. Discourses on Life and Law*. Cambridge, MA: Harvard University Press.
(3) Christian Spoden quoted in Gavan Titley, 2003, *Youth Work with Boys and Young Men as a Means to Prevent Violence in Everyday Life*, Council of Europe, p 23
(4) *Our Bodies – Their Battle Ground: Gender-based Violence in Conflict Zones*. Source: http://www.Irinnews.org/webspecials/GBV/print/p-Definitions.asp
(5) Source: e-mail exchange with Professor Manuela Martinez on 19 and 25 July, 2005
(6) Testimony of a young Hungarian domestic violence victim – NANE hotline
(7) Travis, A., 'Both sexes equally likely to suffer domestic violence' in *The Guardian*, 22 January 1999. (p.12).
(8) Source: http://www.homeoffice.gov.uk/rds/pdfs/hors191.pdf,
(9) Source: http://www.homeoffice.gov.uk/rds/pdfs04/hors276.pdf
(10) Ferree, M.M., (2004, September). 'Assessing the science: key issues for research on violence against women'. Paper presented at the Conference *Everyday violence and human rights* in Osnabrück, Germany.
(11) Source: http://www.who.int/gender/violence/en
(12) Source: http://www.womenaid.org/press/info/humanrights/warburtonfull.htm#Scale of the problem
(13) Source: http://www.unifem.org/filesconfirmed/149/213_chapter01.pdf
(14) Parliamentary Assembly of the Council of Europe. (2002). *Domestic Violence against Women*, Recommendation 1582. Adopted 27 September, 2002
(15) Amnesty International. (2004). 'It's in our hands. Stop violence against women'.
(16) Source: http://www.rip.org.uk/elearning/eproject/project1/pg1.asp
(17) Testimony of a man who works for the gay NGO New Age / Rainbow in Novi Sad, Serbia.
(18) Domestic violence victim, NANE hotline, Hungary
(19) Donnely, J., Sovereignty and International Intervention: the Case of Human Rights" in Lions, G., &. Mastanduno, M. (Eds.). *Beyond Westphalia? State Sovereignty and International Intervention*. Baltimore and London: John Hopkins University Press (p.122).
(20 *Convention on the Elimination of All Forms of Discrimination Against Women (CEDAW)*, Dec. 18, 1979, 1249 U.N.T.S. 13, 19 I.L.M. 33 (entered into force Sept. 3, 1981).
(21) CEDAW, Article 1
(22) Keck, M.E., & Sikkink K. (1998). *Activists Beyond Borders. Advocacy Networks in International Politics*. Ithaca and London: Cornell University Press. (p.168).
(23) *United Nations Declaration on the Elimination of Violence against Women (DEVAW)*, General Assembly Resolution 48/104, 20 December 1993
(24) Lentin, A. (2004). 'The problem of culture and human rights in the response to racism', in Titley, G. (Ed.) *Resituating Culture*. Strasbourg: Council of Europe Publishing. For a full discussion see Lentin, A. (2004). *Racism and Anti-Racism in Europe*. London: Pluto Press.
(25) *United Nations Declaration on the Elimination of Violence against Women (DEVAW)*, General Assembly Resolution 48/104, 20 December 1993 Article 2 (a).
(26) Donnelly, J., (1999). 'Non-Discrimination and Sexual Orientation: Making a place for sexual minorities in the global human rights regime', in Baehr, P., Flinterman, C. & Senders, M. (Eds.), *Innovation and Inspiration: Fifty Years of the Universal Declaration of Human Rights*. Amsterdam: Royal Netherlands Academy of Arts and Sciences. (pp.93-110).
(27) Copelon, R., (1994). 'Understanding Domestic Violence as Torture' in Cook, R. (Ed.). *Human Rights of Women. National and International Perspectives*. Philadelphia: University of Pennsylvania Press. (p.116- 152).
(28) Nane Hotline, Hungary
(29) Copelon: p.128-129
(30) Excerpted from www.gmdvp.org and LAMBDA Gay and Lesbian Anti Violence Project (El Paso).
(31) Source: http://www.gmdvp.org/pages/dennis.html
(32) Source: http://www.vawnet.org/NRCDVPublications/TAPE/Papers/NRC_camp-full.php
(33) 3: Mobilising against gender inequality and gender-based violence

3. Mobilising against gender inequality and gender-based violence

3.1 Gender in youth work: perspectives and challenges

How can gender play a role in youth work? What are the benefits of working with gender?

Where there are people, there are gender issues and the potential for gender-based violence. This implies that when young people work, organise, socialise and educate together, gendered dimensions of youth work are ever-present and must be taken seriously. This chapter examines the roles gender may play in youth work, the importance of gender equality and gender mainstreaming in youth work, projects and organisations, and, finally, examines different expressions of gender based violence in youth contexts. This chapter concludes by presenting some practical ways to mobilise against gender-based violence. We hope that the pragmatic approach of this chapter will encourage you to take specific actions in your work. With this pragmatic dimension, however, comes a strong emphasis on reflection: working with gender and issues of identity, power and safety in groups of young people is a sensitive and demanding task. This chapter contains a strong 'training for trainers' element as it considers the kinds of reflections on experience, competences and ethics that all people who work with youth should engage with.

Youth work often aims to increase the participation of young people in society, or to support young people with a certain interest, objective or hobby. Most youth organisations and networks in Europe have formal and informal practices of democracy, which are based in a commitment to the equal treatment of individuals. To involve gender equality in this work is therefore not a huge logical leap. Organisations or projects that specifically work on human rights, citizenship, active participation, minority youth, intercultural learning, anti-racism or anti-discrimination - to name just a few work areas – are intrinsically involved.

Despite this, it is worth asking how often gender is an explicit topic in youth work, training and organisation, for a number of reasons. Gender issues may be considered the work of specialised organisations. People may maintain that there are no gender issues to deal with. For some, gender conjures up images of feminism and 'yesterday's politics'. Given that gender is often equated with women's issues, it is often the case that it is dealt with in special girls' groups. And sometimes you may even hear that 'there are more important things to be dealt with.' This is a lost opportunity. Young people can instigate change by taking charge of change and by changing themselves. While many gendered patterns of inequality persist in our societies, youth work is known to be willing to challenge old structures and to break new ground, and many young people are engaged in different kinds of projects related to gender equality.

gender matters

While there are also youth organisations whose work is solely devoted to this issue, recognising and tackling problems and discrimination that happen in one's own context is a challenge no credible youth organisation should avoid.

3.1.1 Gender in youth work practices

What different ways of working with gender exist? What does it mean to work, for example, with girls or boys groups?

Returning to the question of implicit and explicit work on gender in youth work, you may be aware of, or involved in, areas of youth work that consider gender as integral to their practice. Below are some areas where gender issues are central to youth work practice:

Gender as a human rights issue

> For further discussion about gender and human rights, see "COMPASS, a manual on human rights education with young people", p 354, (http://www.coe.int/compass)

Many youth organisations work on human rights. Gender equality is an integral part of human rights, and therefore this work is fundamental to human rights work or human rights education. This relationship implies that human rights workers or educators should be knowledgeable about gender issues and gender in-equality, and have the competencies to address them. Conversely, working on gender issues with young people is also an important approach for preventing human rights violations and for strengthening human rights education.

Preventative work

In a world of multiple priorities, preventative work often has difficulties in proving its importance because other pressing issues and problems that manifest themselves attract more attention. Nevertheless, youth work and activism are central to preventative educational work in many ways. In Europe, anti-racism education and conflict and violence prevention work have proven that much can be gained through recognising potential problems and addressing them before they become out of control. Working preventively with gender issues may puzzle some people because prevention involves addressing issues before they become problems. As a youth trainer working with a gender equality project in Sweden described: "When we started the girls group and the boys group at the school, many teachers questioned the need for it. They seemed to question the need to address issues of violence when no-one had been hurt." However as working with young people on these issues develops, many of these questions are answered. Specific issues may surface, and more generally, the fact that gendered ideas and stereotypes are so ingrained in society implies that all of us carry them to some extent. A key idea in preventative work is that knowledge can bring action. Knowing that discrimination and violence based on gender take place invites everyone to be an agent of change. Preventative work, in many social and cultural climates, is forced to argue a case for its necessity and effectiveness. When gender does not seem to be a pressing issue, and where preventative work has difficulty in producing measurable results, it is crucial to base programmes on good research and background material, and to argue that since results may take years to chart, programmes require follow-up and comparisons with similar environments without preventive work.

There are various approaches to preventative work in relation to gender. Preventative work should not be understood only negatively, in terms of stopping something from happening, but also positively, as spaced and experiences that allow reflection and personal development.

Compensatory pedagogy

Compensatory pedagogy in gender equality work means focusing specifically on behaviour that is traditionally discouraged by gender stereotypes and assumptions. It aims to give everyone the possibility to develop different kinds of behaviours holistically. For example, both boys and girls are subject to many pressurising messages about sex, intimacy and sexual behaviour. Kruse [1] points out that a holistic picture of a person means the possibility for both autonomy and intimacy. According to Kruse, the general aim for work with girls is to develop autonomy, and for work with boys to develop intimacy. The general aims of compensatory pedagogy can be explained as follows:
- to offer girls and boys the same possibilities for personal development, happiness and challenges;
- to provide a learning environment where girls and boys can broaden their experiences without being limited by traditional gender roles;
- to support girls and boys, - through increased self awareness – to choose their own future according to their own wish and interests;
- to contribute to the development of positive sexual identities. [2]

Work with single sex groups

Single sex groups are a good example of compensatory pedagogy, and have emerged as a way to invite girls and boys to reflect among themselves on what it means to be a girl/young woman or a boy/young man. It works in single-sex arrangements to provide the possibility for comfort, intimacy and a freedom from assumptions and images which may pressurise or distract. These groups help bridge the gap between societal expectations and self-actualisation. A well functioning girls' or boys' group can also provide members with a feeling of belonging, with tools to deal with problems and conflicts that arise in everyday life, and with increased self-awareness.

However, a girls' group or a boys' group is not just a group of girls and boys. Planned educational programmes are important, and it is essential that youth leaders know the shared aims of the group they are working with and can select and adapt methods accordingly. Working with groups of girls/young women may have very different emphases than working with boys/young men. However similar questions about identity, roles and relationships may occur, and, thus, exercises and facilitative methods can often be used with minor adaptation.

Reflection

What does leading a single sex group involve? The following guidelines provide the basis for reflection.

- Make sure you know your own reasons and motivations for being involved. This is especially important if the validity of the work is questioned, or if you become unsure about your own involvement.
- Make sure you have reflected on your own beliefs and assumptions concerning gender. A good leader does not try to be perfect, but instead demonstrates their own ongoing reflection. This is important because you are likely to become a role model because of your position.
- Accept that working with gender issues requires competences. These competences include considering issues of gender, identity and power in society, being at ease with potentially difficult topics - such as sexuality – that may arise, and the ability to facilitate groups and implement youth activities. Working with gender requires training, and those interested, as well as their organisations, should regard this as an important responsibility.
- Ensure that there are guidelines for participation in the group and support for you for dealing with what is disclosed in the group. For example, participants should know that you need to act upon reports of abuse or violence that are illegal and harmful.
- Realise the limits of this kind of work. A girls or boys group is not a therapy group, and the most you can do is advise somebody on specialised support if they feel they need it.
- Emphasise, even in single sex groups, that women and men have much in common. Talking about the 'opposite sex' may reinforce stereotypes of opposing natures and behaviours.

Setting up a group:

- A girls'/boys' group can be organised as project group within wider projects, organisations, clubs or networks. A set period allows people to enter out of curiosity within a clear time frame, and provides a sense of momentum. A common framework involves a meeting time of 1-2 hours a week for approximately 10 weeks.
- A girls'/boys' group should not be too big. If it consists of 8-12 people it will allow for confidence building and personal exchange.
- In a youth club there could also be a group as a constant feature or permanent time of the week.
- You can also choose to have an open group with new members coming from time to time, although methods and approaches would have to be adjusted to this lack of continuity.

3.2 Gender mainstreaming in youth training and youth projects

Why is it important to mainstream gender into youth work?

As was pointed out in the introduction, this resource has been developed in response to an observation that gender is regarded as an issue that has been 'solved' when it hasn't been; it is also the case that gender is not regularly included (on the agenda) in youth work, or if it is, that it is insufficiently integrated and developed within a youth training context. For example, have you ever heard a youth worker, leader or trainer speaking about, or being asked about, their competences for working with gender? Non-discrimination and equality regardless of gender, sexual orientation, ethnicity, class and beliefs is a fundamental basis for participatory work; however, each of these areas needs its own specific approaches. This is where 'gender mainstreaming' is relevant: Gender mainstreaming does not mean simply counting numbers of young women and young men to ensure equal numbers, nor does it demand having special activities for these groups, although these can be part of it (see 3.1.1). This section explores gender mainstreaming and how it can benefit a youth organisation or network.

3.2.1 Gender mainstreaming

What does gender mainstreaming mean?

Gender mainstreaming involves incorporating equal opportunities for women and men into all policies and activities of an organisation. According to the United Nations' Economic and Social Council,

> *Mainstreaming a gender perspective is the process of assessing the implications for women and men of any planned action, including legislation, policies or programmes, in all areas and at all levels. It is a strategy for making women's as well as men's concerns and experiences an integral dimension of the design, implementation, monitoring and evaluation of policies and programmes in all political, economic and societal spheres so that women and men benefit equally and inequality is not perpetuated. The ultimate goal is to achieve gender equality.*

This can also be simplified as the idea of 'gender glasses', namely routinely adopting a perspective in youth activities, projects or training that examines the nature of the opportunities provided for comfortable and meaningful participation.

Wearing 'gender glasses' could mean examining any of the following issues:

Decision-making

Who are in the decision-making structures of the organisation?

Are both men and women actively involved in decision making?[15]

Do structures or dominant attitudes need to be changed to promote equal participation for women and men?

Does the decision taken affect women and men differently?

---

15 For example a new database, launched by the European Commission, on women and men in decision-making confirms that women are still far from taking an equal part in the decision-making process generally, but their position is better in some countries and in some sectors.
Source: http://europa.eu.int/comm/employment_social/women_men_stats/index_en.htm

Activities

Who are the different target groups of our activities?

How do we address them?

Does the nature of the activity allow for equal participation for girls and boys? Are there any factors to be taken into account?

Are we ready to address gender as an important issue in our society, whether we believe it is an issue in our organisation or not?

Attitudes and language

How are women and men referred to? Do we reflect on the ways we represent images of gender roles? Is there verbal harassment within the organisation?

Do we refer to an unknown participant or youth worker as 'he' or 'she', or do we use inclusive language ('she or he', 'he or she') or avoid personal pronouns?

Do task roles tend to be automatically distributed according to traditional notions of gender roles?

Approach and Analysis

What assumptions and ideas guide your organisation's treatment of gender and in-/equality?

Have you considered how social relationships concerning gender and power may influence your organisation?

3.2.2 Gender mainstreaming and gender equality

What is the relationship between mainstreaming and policy?

It is important to consider gender mainstreaming as a complement, rather than substitute for 'traditional' gender equality policies. They are two different strategies to reach the same goal.

The main difference between mainstreaming and specific gender equality policies is the actors involved and the policies that are chosen to be addressed. Equality policies address specific problems resulting from gender inequality, and this policy is then implemented on a national or organisational level. A common European example of this is laws designed to protect equal opportunities for employment.

The starting point for mainstreaming, however, is when a policy already exists. Mainstreaming involves putting on the glasses that examine the ways in which the policy is working or not working, and the ways in which the goals of the policy can be enhanced through re-organisation and change. Mainstreaming sees the policy as a specific implement in a larger context.

Mainstreaming is a fundamental strategy - it may take some time before it is implemented, but it has a potential for a sustainable change. 'Traditional' forms of equality policy can have more rapid results, but they are usually limited to specific policy areas. Gender mainstreaming builds upon knowledge and lessons learnt from former experiences with equality policies. However, mainstreaming cannot function optimally within the legal and institutional frameworks of 'traditional' equality policy, nor can it be as direct and specific as gender equality policies. Mainstreaming and specific equality policies are not only dual and complementary strategies; they work hand in hand with each other.

3.2.3 Guidelines and instruments for gender mainstreaming.

What can I do practically to mainstream gender?

Strategies and policies

A policy document contains (a) statements of principle in regard to gender equality (b) specific regulations if any, and how these will be monitored and (c) how gender equality should be safeguarded.

The drafting of strategies and policies to promote gender equality can prove to be an important process in itself, even before the strategy or policy is implemented. This is because the strategies and policies of an organisation or club should be based on a shared analysis of the situation, and how it can be changed. In participatory environments, such processes and documents need to be dynamic, and open to consultation and revision. A strategy document can contain points of action to be taken to promote gender equality. These action points could include the development of awareness raising events, policies for the election of board and committee members, and a review of the activities and resources used and produced by the organisation. It is important that any such strategy be periodically evaluated.

Awareness-raising

Awareness-raising can take many forms, but aims to address people's attitudes and knowledge. Although sexism, discrimination and gender-based violence cannot be addressed by knowledge alone, accurate and relevant information, and the possibility to engage with a range of perspective on these issues is very important. While opponents of gender mainstreaming often suggest that 'awareness-raising' creates problems from nowhere, women may not realise that what is happening to them is discrimination if they are used to being treated in a discriminatory manner. Similarly, men may feel uncomfortable with dominant masculine norms and wonder if something is wrong with them. To start to talk about gender roles can help people to move out of restrictive roles and to define who they are for themselves. Raising awareness about violence and discrimination can mobilise people to take action. This includes organisations and politicians. Campaigns, projects, training courses, demonstrations, special committees or other instruments can be tools for awareness-raising.

Sex quotas

Proactively ensuring balanced ratios between men and women is a practice based on a belief that gender equality is best achieved through a proactive approach where certain regulations are needed to promote equal treatment. It can mean that a board of an organisation could contain maximum 60% of either men or women. It could mean that participants for an activity are selected according to a 50-50 ratio of the sexes.

Integration

Integrating gender equality awareness to all actions, activities and policies of an organisation is central to the philosophy of mainstreaming. It implies that instead of having a special committee responsible for initiating and monitoring gender issues, this is seen as the responsibility of all committees. The responsibility to safeguard equality would vanish because it is dealt with in a specific committee.

Reflection

Checklist for implementing gender mainstreaming [3]
- Adequate research: Do you have information on the situation in your organisation? Do you have gender-specific statistics on members, members of the board, delegates to important events, and organisational responsibilities?
- Legitimation: Is gender equality on the agenda of your organisation's governing bodies?
- Strategy-building: Have you developed a strategy for your work? Will it include courses, workshops or seminars? Is there a need for specific policies?
- Transversal implementation: Do the organisation's plan, budget and evaluation have a gender equality perspective? Is gender awareness an issue for all staff and board members and integrated into activities?

3.2.4 Gender mainstreaming in training

As a trainer, what can I do? How does gender mainstreaming effect training?

Any kind of training course or learning activity can apply a gender mainstreaming approach, whatever the subject is. As a leader, or participant, you can be observant of patterns of behaviour among men and women and address them. By your own actions and attitude you can create an awareness of the fact that men and women are equal in value and to challenge assumptions and norms by being conscious, for example, of the language you use, examples you choose, and the role models you refer to. As a youth leader you have an important role to play in the promotion of gender equality. Knowledge and awareness of this issue is vital for the execution of democratic leadership.

Gender is a transversal issue in training; thus, any kind of session can have an explicit focus on gender. For example: How does an outreach campaign involve or reach both boys and girls? What is the gender dimension of an intercultural youth project? How should a trainer involved in Euro-Mediterranean youth work address gender issues? What role does gender play in an anti-racist campaign? How do you apply a gender analysis to conflict transformation? This kind of approach makes the gender dimension visible without having to limit it to a session on 'gender'. Of course, there is always a gender dimension to activities, but ignoring it in the planning and implementation of these activities may leave out part of your target group, reinforce stereotypes or just simply miss an opportunity to address a central aspect of human rights and participation.

It may rarely be necessary to have single-sex sessions on a training course as a strategy for inclusion, unless the subject matter and cultural context suggests that it would be more sensitive to do so. More generally the idea is to have a diversity of methods and activities and to make information inclusive so that both men and women feel included.

Reflection

Guiding questions that could be used in relation to gender mainstreaming and training:
- Is there a policy on gender balance in the training teams? How has this developed and how is it implemented? Is this policy applied to external guests such as lecturers or workshop leaders?
- Is gender a central aspect of discussion for the team in relation to their teamwork and their educational activities?
- Is gender balance a criterion for choosing participants? What are the reasons for this?
- Do methods and methodologies facilitate equal participation?
- Do sessions and approaches specifically address the issue of gender and equality? If not, why not?

Gender is a traversal aspect of every important focus in youth work training in Europe. Most obviously, gender could be an aspect of, or the focus of, a **human rights education training.** Discrimination and unequal treatment due to sex are breaches of human rights. Consequently, all human rights can be discussed in relation to gender. Trainers who are aware of this can, for example, introduce a gender perspective into a session through questions in an exercise debriefing. Similarly, gender awareness in **project planning** and **project management** training could encourage making an analysis of how the project and activities may apply and affect young women and men in the target group; an initial needs analysis for a project can also feature a gender aspect.

Since gender roles affect us in our personal lives you may want to put extra time into creating emotional safety in the group and make sure that there are common rules that the group agrees on. As trainers it is important that you share among yourselves your own ideas and feelings about the subject. It is also recommended that you know what triggers you to step out of your role, and how you should handle such situations.

3.2.5 Ethics and competence in gender training

What should I be aware of when training on gender and gender-based violence?

Ethical considerations belong in any training activity that brings people together, and these ethical considerations are heightened when issues of identity and power are present. A primary ethical consideration for trainers is sharing amongst themselves their own ideas and feelings, and being aware of how different issues trigger one's emotions and beliefs. Working on this awareness is the first step towards creating a safe group process. The following aspects are also important:

- Discretion: Issues of gender, identity and especially gender-based violence can be very private. Make sure you allow for security and privacy if there is a chance that people's own experiences may be engaged by a training course.
- Humour: Using humour is often a great way to take away tension or break a deadlock in a discussion. Using humour in discussing gender can be very effective. However, there are millions of jokes referring to gender that are sexist or discriminatory. Think through the humour you are using and how you will react to sexist jokes in relation to what you know about the group.
- Responsibility: It is important to recognise that general discussions and reflections may bring personal issues that are beyond the competence of a trainer or training course. For example, issues of gender-based violence are often regarded as criminal acts. You and your organisation need to have a policy on how you potentially report such issues to the police and/or to parents.

These ethical points raise a wider question about the kinds of competence educators and youth leaders need to develop. As chapter one discusses, our gendered identity and socialisation are powerful, and provide us with many common sense aspects of our sense of self and roles in society. How much people 'feel to be' their sex or what is expected of their sex is individual. But none of us escape the issue of sex and gender. Therefore, each of us has an experience and probably an opinion on a range of gender issues. We are all free to engage in debates or organise activities or write articles on the issue of gender. What we should know as youth workers and trainers, however, is that gender is a well-resourced, studied and researched competence area. In academic fields such as sociology, anthropology, human rights, biology and medicine specific or integrated fields of sex and gender analysis have emerged. Many universities have special institutes of gender studies. Feminist theory is a popular discourse and a research area. Local and international NGOs and institutions conduct in-depth studies on gender equality and gender-based violence. If you want to work seriously with the issue of gender you need to do some background research and know when to consult different expertise or experience. The fact that we are all gendered does not mean that gender is just a question of opinion.

> **Reflection**
>
> The following points offer some suggestions for reflecting on working with gender and young people:
> - Think through your own opinion and question it regularly
> - Search for and study material on the issue of your interest, and for material that questions or contradicts your findings or your opinions. Gender is a much disputed area!
> - Compare how gender norms may differ according to the context.
> - Be aware of the gender equality legislation in your country, and of the international treaties and declarations that promote gender equality.
> - Start talking to colleagues and friends about gender. What do they think of issues you have confronted?
> - Observe how people around you speak of men, women and gender roles
> - Observe your own behaviour towards baby boys and baby girls, teenage boys and teenage girls, and adult women and adult men; do you feel or behave differently? Why?
> - Put on your gender glasses while reading your newspaper; how are people portrayed on photos and described in the text, who has been asked to comment, where do you see women in the paper and where do you see men?

Counteracting domination techniques

How do power relations manifest themselves? What strategies do people use to dominate others?

In training, and in organisational contexts, it is necessary to consider the ways in which power relationships and gender norms are maintained. To highlight and analyse how the relationship between the sexes can be linked to power, the Norwegian social psychologist Berit Ås developed an analysis of domination techniques which discuss the follow

1. Making invisible: If nobody listens to what you say, you can easily stop talking. Marginalising people can be done through individual actions, but also through an environment were it is difficult to make one's voice heard.
2. Ridiculing: Ridicule can be expressed in comments, insults and jokes, or in non-verbal communication that hints at the other's inadequacy. People may often play along with these dynamics to avoid being subject of ridicule.
3. Withholding information: Those who hold important information may exercise power and influence. If information is not shared evenly among people in the same position or situation, or if decisions are taken without involving everyone concerned, there is an inequality of power. It may be that important issues are discussed in informal groups, or that decisions are already taken informally when the official body meets.
4. Double punishment: Double punishment means that whatever you do it is wrong. A girl who is not involved in lots of discussions can be seen as passive, boring and avoiding responsibility. But on the other hand if she gets involved in everything she is said to be taking too much space. A boy who does not want to play football

can be called a sissy. If he decides to join in the next day he might be teased for succumbing to group pressure.

5. Shame and guilt: Creating feelings of shame and guilt is a powerful tool of oppression. Among boys it may mean to make someone seem feminine or not manly enough. Families who exercise excessive control over their children's habits may encourage shame and guilt in their children for causing unrest in the family if they don't obey. Similarly, youth contexts may involve situations where people are shamed for not taking part, or sharing a joke, and so forth.

6. Objectification: We chiefly associate objectification with the kinds of sexualised images that circulate in popular media. However women and men can be objectified in organisational contexts, by being referred to solely according to their physical appearance, or by being included in something as a 'token' rather than on their merits.

7. Violence and the threat of violence: The fear of being subject to violence is a strong factor restricting people's behaviour and freedom of movement. For example, having to take a long route home in order to avoid violence, or not daring to go out at night due to potential violence, are everyday realities for a lot of young people.

3.3 Taking action against gender-based violence

This section discusses how to take action and mobilise against different kinds of gender-based violence.

The different ways in which you mobilise against gender-based violence depend on your target group and the specific objectives you have in mind. Do you aim to reach politicians in order to pressure them to design a legal framework to protect the victims of violence, or do you aim to train youth workers in raising awareness on this issue? In the first case the use of political lobbying may be the best way to mobilise, whereas in the second case a training event may be an appropriate method. Two possible ways of mobilising against gender-based violence are by setting up a project or organising a training course. Look at some of the exercises in the next chapter that will help you identify practical ways to mobilise against gender-based violence.

3.3.1 Identifying whether forms of gender-based violence are present in your organisation or group

How will I know if someone I'm working with is directly experiencing gender-based violence? Should I do something about it or not?

This is a type of preventive action you could take as a youth worker, because victims and survivors (people who have experienced gender-based violence directly) are potentially in *every* group. Documenting incidents of gender-based violence in your organisation is crucial for collecting accurate information, and monitoring incidents of gender-based violence in your organisation (or incidents faced by members of your organisation) is crucial for developing a response to the victims and the perpetrators. However this may largely mean evaluating the climate in which people interact in your organisation.

If there are issues that need to be aired in a group or organisation, effective intervention strategies that are aimed at potential perpetrators, potential victims and survivors need to be designed. It is important that you make this a highly participatory process, where youth group members are centrally involved. Youth work has the potential to really make a difference and in that respect the unique structure of your youth group should also be an object of critical scrutiny: do you offer a safe environment to your group members? Finally, as gender-based violence can in some cases involve criminal violence you need to know the limits of intervention, and when it is advisable to involve specialists from other NGOs, services or even the police.

3.3.2 Youth groups and work in broader coalitions

Do youth workers have a special responsibility to address issues of gender-based violence?

There is a clear need for youth workers to work on these issues in society, and to intervene when they are aware of or faced with gender-based violence. This can be considered both as *preventative* as well as *responsive* work. However, youth groups do not need to operate on their own. They can identify existing specific expertise from other organisations. They can participate in ongoing campaigns. This is particularly important when it comes to providing victims with appropriate support: alliances with organisations working in the fields of health and social protection allow you to point victims in the direction of gender-based violence to experts.

The kind of work youth groups can achieve will also depend on the social-political and legal context in your country: it defines the contours of how successfully you can implement your project or action. For example:
- Is there a widespread social and political acknowledgement that gender-based violence is an issue?
- Is there a law in your country that protects victims of gender-based violence and punishes perpetrators?
- Are these laws successfully applied? What are the enforcing mechanisms and who is collecting the data?

In many countries, regrettably, the perpetrators of some of the violence may be the police or state institutions, and thus they themselves are probably in charge of collecting data; this may deter victims from reporting. It is thus of utmost importance to familiarise yourself with the legal aspects of your nation state.

It is likely that young people's organisations and networks will aim to concentrate on more youth-specific activities, such as publicising a case in local or national media, organising a hearing for young people and inviting politicians, or organising seminars and projects.[16]

A successful public awareness project is the Hungarian organisation NANE's *Silent Witness* project.[17]

Silent Witness Exhibition: NANE Women's Rights Association, Budapest, Hungary

In 1990, an ad hoc group of women artists and writers, upset about the growing number of women in Minnesota being murdered by their partners or acquaintances, joined together with several other women's organizations to form Arts Action Against Domestic Violence. They felt an urgency to do something that would speak out against the escalating domestic violence in their state, something that would commemorate the lives of the 26 women whose lives had been lost in 1990 as a result of domestic violence. After much brainstorming, they decided to create 26 free-standing, life-sized red wooden figures, each one bearing the name of a woman who once lived, worked, had neighbours, friends, family, children, and whose life ended violently at the hands of a husband, ex-husband, partner, or acquaintance. A twenty-seventh figure was added to represent those uncounted women whose murders went unsolved or were erroneously ruled 'accidental'. The organizers called the figures the 'Silent Witnesses'. (For more information, see www.silentwitness.net)

NANE Women's Rights Association launched its Silent Witness project six years ago based on the U.S. project. In 2002 NANE created an exhibition of 40 figures, which was roughly representative of the number of women murdered every year in domestic violence. The aim of the exhibition was also to attract media attention to the story and the issues surrounding it, as paying for advertisements or mass media campaigns is extremely expensive.

The project has lived up to NANE's expectations by bringing in a range of media which would have not been available otherwise: the Silent Witness March and Speak out on November 25, 2002 (on the eve of the International Day of the Elimination of Violence Against Women) was shown on all news programmes that evening, and every daily paper covered the event in the days that followed. Some even used the event to anchor deeper coverage in their following weekend issue.

Endnotes to Chapter 3

(1) JämO. (2000) *XY XX JämOs handbok mot könsmobbning i skolan*. Stockholm: Jämställdhetsombudsmannen. (p.77).

(2) Kruse, A-M. in JämO. (2000) in *XY XX JämOs handbok mot könsmobbning i skolan*. Stockholm: Jämställdhetsombudsmannen. (pp.77-82).

(3) The Swedish National Board for Youth Affairs. (2003). *Shortcuts to Gender Equality (*adapted).

---

16 For a more in-depth description of project methodology please consult the Project Management T-Kit available online at www.training-youth.net

17 More information can be found at www.nane.hu

4. Exercises addressing gender and gender-based violence with young people

4.1 Working with gender and gender-based violence in the context of (non-formal) education with young people

The aim of "GENDER MATTERS" is to provide information, perspectives and resources for deepening and focusing the emphasis of youth and educational activities which address issues related to gender and gender-based violence within the framework of human rights education.

While there is no special starting point, and it is our intention that you have the opportunity to choose the parts that are relevant for you, we strongly recommend you look through the whole manual to gain an overall picture of the contents, and that you read the parts of the conceptual chapters most closely related to the issues being addressed by your work with young people. The previous chapters cover conceptual and definitional information on gender and gender-based violence, as well as information relevant for mobilising to combat gender-based violence and human rights abuses related to gender.

As already outlined in the introduction to the manual, reading this resource, and thinking about its use in relation to your youth work, must be accompanied by consideration of questions of responsibility, ethics and sensitivity:

- This resource does not expect prior expertise from readers. However, it is based on the principle that while gender is of relevance to everyone, it does not follow that running safe and ethical explorations of gender in youth work is straightforward. Specific training reflections, approaches and methodologies are necessary, and a sensitive approach to dealing with disclosures that participants may make in the context of such activities is required.
- Working with gender – as with other special topics in the context of human rights education – is a *competence area*. It always begins with the youth activist working with him- or herself, and reflecting on the attitudes, beliefs, knowledge and behaviour that he or she brings to youth work in general, and work on gender in particular.
- As with COMPASS[1], users do not have to read this manual in its entirety to be able to use it. How much a user reads (and reflects on) before using the exercises is guided by how competent they feel about their own self-reflection and the needs of their group. But it goes without saying that using this resource should be preceded by a reflection on just how competent one is to use the exercises proposed.
- This manual asks those who read it to be translators, not necessarily from one language to another, but from one context to another. Those working with the

---

[1] www.coe.int/compass

resources developed in the manual, and especially in this chapter, will have to supplement the information provided with information from, for example, their own national institutions, NGOs and local contexts. In addition, it is important for users to decide where different perspectives do not fit their experience and youth work context, and to adapt and substitute examples, ideas and explanations.

- Finally, working on gender, sex, gender-based violence and related issues is an essential part of all youth work because it is something that concerns all young people. The questions and concepts that are addressed through this work are ones that are relevant to young people's lives and relate directly to the world they live in. This is why these issues have to be addressed and in a way in which young people have the chance to explore them themselves.

4.2 Human rights education - an educational approach

Before you work with these activities, it is important to understand the educational approach within which the manual and the activities included in this chapter have been developed, namely human rights education. The underlying approach to human rights education is the same as the one outlined in COMPASS, and for the users less familiar with COMPASS, there are a few points, in particular, worth reading.

Human rights education is about education for change, both personal and social. It is about developing young people's competence to be active citizens who participate in their communities to promote and protect human rights. The focus is the educational process of developing knowledge, skills, values and attitudes that are relevant for acting positively on behalf of human rights, and specifically in the area of gender related human rights or when gender-based violence is concerned.

Human rights education can, therefore, be defined as

- ...educational programmes and activities that focus on promoting equality in human dignity, in conjunction with other programmes such as those promoting intercultural learning, participation and empowerment of minorities.[2]

In this process we:

- start from what people already know, from their opinions and experiences, and from this base enable them to search for, and discover together, new ideas and experiences;
- encourage the participation of young people to contribute to discussions and to learn from each other as much as possible;
- encourage people to translate their learning into simple but effective actions that demonstrate their rejection of injustice, inequality and violations of human rights.

---

2   Official definition of Human Rights Education by the Council of Europe Youth Programme (Directorate of Youth and Sport).

4.2.1 Knowledge, skills, attitudes and values supporting human rights education

In order for young people to work in the defence of human rights and towards a deeper understanding of human rights issues, they need certain kinds of knowledge and skills. They also need to develop relevant attitudes and values. In terms of knowledge, young people need to develop an understanding of the main concepts and the historical development of human rights, as well as the standards demanded by the main instruments and mechanisms for human rights protection. This means knowing about one's own rights and the way they interact with other people's rights, as well as how to defend one's own rights and those of others. In terms of skills, young people need to be able to communicate about and advocate for human rights in public and private, to critically assess situations in terms of human rights and reflect on what constitutes an abuse of human rights, to deal with conflict and learn to transform it in a constructive manner, and to take an active and constructive role in their communities. Finally, in terms of attitudes and values, young people need to be committed to the protection of human dignity, to develop empathy and solidarity for others and to acquire a sense of justice and responsibility for their own actions and those of others.

Knowing about human rights, gender issues and gender-based violence is very important, but not enough to ensure that young people are able to contribute constructively to the defence of human rights, especially those related to gender.

It is necessary that young people have a far deeper understanding about how these human rights evolve out of people's needs and why they have to be protected. For example, young people with no direct experience of gender-based violence may think that the issue is of no concern to them. From a human rights perspective this position is not acceptable. People everywhere have a responsibility to protect the human rights of others, including those related to gender. It does not matter whether the right to life or freedom to determine one's own reproductive future is under discussion. Human rights are about democratic values, respect and tolerance. Educational activities which aim to address gender related human rights must create a learning environment that respects these values.

Human rights issues, including those which are gender related, are controversial because different people have different value systems and therefore see rights and responsibilities in different ways. These differences, which manifest themselves as conflicts of opinion, are the basis of our educational work.

Two important aims of human rights education are
- to equip young people with the skills of appreciating - but not necessarily agreeing with - different points of view about an issue;
- to help young people to develop skills in finding mutually agreeable solutions to problems.

This manual and its activities are based on an understanding that conflicts of opinion can be used constructively for the learning process, provided that the facilitator feels confident in addressing possible conflicts in a group. As in many non-formal educational activities, the purpose is not so much that everyone agrees with a given result, but rather that the participants can also learn from that process (e.g. listening to each other, expressing themselves, respecting differences of opinion, etc.).

4.2.2 Experiential learning – a basis for human rights education

These competencies, especially the skills and values of communication, critical thinking, advocacy, tolerance and respect, cannot be taught: they have to be learned through experience. This is why all the activities included in this chapter promote co-operation, participation and learning through experience, in addition to treating the sensitive issues around gender and gender-based violence. We aim to encourage young people to think, feel and act, and to engage their heads, hearts and hands in the defence of gender related human rights.

Cooperation, experience and participation are all essential to the activities that we propose in this manual. Learning in these activities takes place because the young people who participate in them have the chance to cooperate with each other during the learning process, to have an experience they can analyse in light of the realities they would like to change and to participate actively in the learning process. These activities demand participation and involvement so that the people doing them gain an experience through which they learn not only with their heads but also with their hearts and hands. These sorts of activities are sometimes called 'games' because they are fun and people play them with enthusiasm. We prefer to use the term 'exercise' because it expresses the fact that such activities are not 'just for fun', but they are purposeful means to achieve educational aims.

For this reason, the exercises proposed in this manual have been developed in respect of the 'experiential learning cycle'[3]. It is not sufficient to simply 'do' an activity (phase 1 of the learning cycle). It is essential to follow through with debriefing and evaluation to enable people to reflect on what happened (phase 2), to evaluate their experience (phases 3 & 4) and to go on to decide what to do next (phase 5). In this way they come round to phase 1 of the next cycle in the learning process. In a school setting, activities can help break down artificial barriers between subjects and provide ways of extending links between subject and interest areas to promote a more holistic approach to an issue. In a non-formal educational setting, activities can awaken interest in issues and, because they promote learning in a non-didactic way, they are often intrinsically more acceptable to young people.

The following exercises offer a framework and structure to group experiences, allowing you to work within the limits of your own and the young peoples' experience and compe-

---

3 For further information on the experiential learning cycle and on the steps to learning that are entailed in its five phases, we suggest you consult the following general non-formal education and youth work facilitation resources: T-kit - Training Essentials – www.training-youth.net and COMPASS – www.coe.int/compass The 'experiential learning cycle' – Kolb.

tencies. When carefully facilitated, such activities are an effective method of learning within a task-orientated setting.

4.2.3 Facilitating human rights education in various settings.

In this manual we use the word 'facilitators' for the people who prepare, present and co-ordinate the exercises for participants. A facilitator is someone who helps people discover how much knowledge they already have, who encourages them to learn more and helps them explore their own potential. Facilitation means creating an environment in which people learn, experiment, explore and grow. It is a process of sharing, of giving and taking. It is not a question of one person, who is 'an expert', giving knowledge and skills to others. You may find it helpful to reflect on your own style and practice in order to develop your facilitation skills, especially if you are not yet experienced in dealing with issues related to gender or gender-based violence in the educational work you do with young people.

This manual and the exercises it proposes can be used in extra-curricular activities, on a training course or a seminar, at a summer camp, in a work camp, in a youth club or with a youth group that meets regularly. They can also be used at school in a classroom. They can even be used if you work mostly with adults. Nevertheless, the educational approach and the types of activities described in this manual may seem easier to apply in the non-formal sector than in the formal sector. We believe, however, that the exercises can be useful in both.

4.3 Using the exercises

4.3.1 Choosing exercises

This chapter compiles exercises for training and facilitation that cover different gender issues and aspects of gender-based violence.

Some of the exercises will be similar or close to other exercises that you or your group may already be familiar with. In general, the exercises have been newly developed or adapted from previous experiences or publications. If an exercise has been adapted and the source is known, it has been stated at the beginning of the activity.

You should choose activities that are at the right level for you and your group and that will fit into the time you have. Read the activity through carefully at least twice and try to imagine how the group may react and some of the things they will say. Make sure you have all the materials you will need. Check that there will be enough space, especially if the participants will be breaking up for small-group work.

Again we emphasise that the instructions for each activity are only guidelines and that you should use the material in the way that suits your own needs. Indeed, it is not possible to write activities that will exactly suit every situation across Europe. We expect you to adapt the activities. For example, you might take the basic idea from one activity and use a method from another. Each activity is presented in a standard format.

4.3.2 Key to the presentation of the exercises

Level of complexity

Levels 1 to 4 indicate the general level of competency required, in intellectual and emotional terms, for participation and / or the amount of preparation involved, as well as the level of challenge for the participants and facilitator involved in the activity. In general, the two variables go together: level 1 activities need very little preparation and demand little emotional competence from both participants and facilitator, while those activities at level 4 need much more.

Level 1

These are short, simple activities, mostly useful as starters. Energisers and icebreakers fall into this category. Nonetheless, these activities are of value in the way that they make people interact and communicate with each other.

Level 2

These are simple activities designed to stimulate interest in an issue. They do not require prior knowledge of human rights issues or developed personal or group work skills. Many of the activities at this level are designed to help people develop communication and group work skills while at the same time stimulating their interest in human rights.

Level 3

These are longer activities designed to develop deeper understanding and insights into an issue. They demand higher levels of competency in discussion or group work skills.

Level 4

These activities are longer, require good group work and discussion skills, concentration and co-operation from the participants and also take longer to prepare for. They are also more embracing in that they provide a wider and deeper understanding of the issues.

Overview and themes

This gives brief information about the type of activity and the issues addressed, including any themes that are focused on during the activity.

Group size

This indicates the ideal number of people (including minimum and maxiumum) needed in order to do the activity.

Time

This is the estimated time in minutes needed to complete the whole activity, including the (pre- and / or post-activity) discussion.

Objectives

These outline the learning the exercise hopes to achieve for participants in terms of knowledge, skills, attitudes and values.

Materials

This is a list of equipment needed to run the exercise.

Preparation

This is a list of things the facilitator needs to do or prepare before starting the exercise.

Instructions

This is a list of instructions for how to run the exercise.

Debriefing and evaluation

This section includes suggested questions to help the facilitator to conduct the debriefing and to evaluate the activity (phase 2-4 of the experiential learning cycle).

Tips for facilitators

These include guidance notes, things to be aware of, especially for the debriefing of the activity, information on possible variations in running the activity, and extra background information relevant to the activity or where to find more information on the themes addressed by the exercise.

Suggestions for follow-up

These include ideas for what to do next and links to other activities that are relevant for dealing with the theme.

Ideas for action

These include suggestions, relating to the issues and themes addressed, for next steps to take action on.

Handouts

These include role cards, action pages, background reading material, discussion cards, other materials that should be given to participants in the context of the exercise, etc.

4.3.3 Advice for the facilitation of the exercises presented in this manual

As explained above, we use the term 'facilitators' to describe the role of the people (trainers, teachers, youth workers, peer educators, youth volunteers) who prepare and run the exercises. This terminology helps to emphasise that educational work on the themes of gender and gender-based violence requires a democratic and participative approach. We assume that you are facilitating groups of young people, for example in a classroom, in a youth club, on a training course, at a youth camp or at a seminar.

What follows are both general facilitation tips for work with any kind of youth group and specific advice for working with the highly sensitive issues addressed by GENDER MATTERS. Many different approaches to facilitation exist. All require sensitivity to the contexts of the participants and to their special situations and needs. All can be adapted to specific circumstances with a little effort. However, the facilitation of groups dealing with issues of gender and especially gender-based violence requires particular sensitivity.

In this section, we also address the specificity of facilitation within distinct forms of youth work that are appropriate for working on such issues, such as youth work with young boys or girls and single sex youth work.

Running exercises on sensitive issues such as gender-based violence

Ethical considerations belong in any educational activity that brings people together, and these ethical considerations are heightened when issues of identity and power are present, as in the case of many of the activities dealing with gender or gender-based violence. We therefore strongly suggest that before undertaking activities dealing with gender based violence you read section 3.2.5 of this manual, entitled 'Ethics and competence in gender training'. It will provide you with valuable advice and useful guidelines for dealing with this sensitive topic in an appropriate manner with participants of your educational activity. We also suggest that you take time to read and understand section 1.2.3 of this manual, as it will help to put such ethical considerations in context in relation to the broader issue of gender.

In addition, there are several important issues to take into consideration when beginning to work with the issue of gender and gender-based violence with groups of young people, and in particular when making decisions on which exercises from this manual to choose:

Gender is a politically sensitive issue

Gender related issues and problems in society can be a highly charged political issue. Issues such as equal rights for Lesbian, Gay, Bisexual and Transgender (LGBT) people or the rights of young women to determine their reproductive destinies have caused significant and often acrimonious debates in the public and political sphere between people of different political persuasions, as well as between people of different cultural and social backgrounds. Closer to home, persons of authority surrounding young people (parents, teachers and professional youth workers, for example) may have objections to certain issues being discussed or raised in the context of youth work or leisure time activities (for example, speaking about sex). You need to be aware of this before beginning to work on the issues with young people and when choosing the exercises from this manual that you want to use in your youth group. You also have to make sure that your organisation supports you and that its policies and approaches are not in contradiction with the work you want to do.

Cultural difference matters, too

The cultural background of the members of the group you are working with on issues of gender and gender-based violence is an important factor in choosing your approach and the exercises you will use. In certain communities, specific gender related issues (such as sex, relationships and sexuality) are taboo and should not be spoken about in public or in mixed-sex settings. Young people who have been brought up in such cultural communities may have difficulties, therefore, to engage in open discussion about such issues directly, especially if members of the other sex are present. In addition, the existence of domestic violence and sexual abuse is often denied in traditional (as well as modern-secular) communities. The socialisation of a given participant in this relation will influence whether they will be willing to discuss or resistant to engaging with the exercises you propose. The importance of cultural background can also, however, be overestimated. Not all young people who come from 'traditional communities' will have difficulties to engage with these issues. A person's social background (e.g. coming from a low-income, low-education background) can often be more relevant to how they deal with sexuality, for example, than religion. But the fact that the young people you work with may come from very diverse cultural and social backgrounds, each of which may have a specific way of dealing with the issues, means that you have to consider the intercultural nature of your group in the development of your educational programmes and in the choice of the exercises you propose.

Different types of youth work can be used for different purposes

Educational work on the subject of gender-based violence and other gender related issues can be conducted in the context of so-called 'general youth work', but it is not the same as doing specific human rights education on the issue of gender with young people. In the first place, you have to consider your own reasons for undertaking to work on the issues in the context of general youth work. What is the relevance and need for addressing such issues in that context? Why do the young people you are working with want to or need to address such issues? What are your educational objectives in undertaking the exploration of such issues? Before you start you have to think about such questions, and the answer to them will lead you to reflect on the kind of youth work that is most effective for your purposes.

You may find, on reflection, that other types of youth work than the 'general' are more effective for your group and its needs, and that it is better to undertake human rights education on issues related to gender in the context of specific target groups. Throughout this manual we have made reference to three specific target groups that this kind of youth work may be conducted with: single-sex groups, LGBT and mixed groups. It is important to consider the way in which you want to form groups, considering your educational objectives at any given time. For example, when wishing to engage the members of your group on the issue of female sexuality, you may consider beginning with work in single-sex groups to try to avoid embarrassment or that participants feel forced into discussing something they do not feel comfortable about with members of the other sex. Chapter 3 of this manual deals specifically with the utility single-sex groups.

Finally, while you may consciously decide to engage in youth work with one or other target group for reasons relating to the specificity of the context you are working in, you also have to consider that you can never fully know 'who is in the room'. For example, even if working with an all female group, you may not be aware of the sexual preferences of all its members. Therefore, you must also take into account that within single-sex and mixed groups, there always exists a modicum of diversity that may complicate the dynamics. Unfortunately, the oppressed and marginalised are not immune to prejudice any more than members of the privileged classes or the majority. The most important thing is to remember that everyone needs to feel comfortable and respected if they are going to engage fully.

Disclosure may take place

Noting that one can never fully know 'who is in the room', one will also acknowledge that there is no guarantee whatsoever that a given participant of your activity has not experienced sexual or relationship abuse or another form of gender-based violence. While creating a safe space for participants to discuss sensitive issues related to gender and gender-based violence is of paramount importance to beginning to work on the issues with young people, you have to be prepared for the fact that creating such a safe space may lead young people to 'disclose' a painful past experience of gender-based violence. When this happens, it can be difficult for everyone concerned – the participant disclosing, the other participants and the facilitator.

It is difficult for a facilitator to prepare in advance for dealing with such a situation in the group. The participant may get very emotional, as might other participants listening to their story. Therefore you should consider the following:

- It is imperative not to interrupt or try to stop the participant.
- Make sure you hear the participant through as far as they are willing to go.
- A good way to diffuse the situation is to call for a break and tell everyone to go and freshen up.
- Pay special attention to the participant in question and make sure they are not left alone if they do not want to be. You or another member of the team they trust might accompany them to another room to calm down and freshen up. They may need a short time away from the group, or alone.
- It may be necessary, either immediately or at a later point, to come back to the disclosure and speak about the fact that it took place in the whole group.
- Whatever you and your team decide to do, the decision should be made in consultation with the participant who made the disclosure. This also goes for how the disclosure is to be dealt with in the group.

Finally, disclosure in the context of youth work is not only a matter of dealing with a complicated group dynamic or an emotionally charged situation. When a participant discloses an experience they have had, the act of which constituted a crime (rape, sexual abuse, grievous bodily harm), then you may be obliged to inform the relevant authorities (police, social services, etc). You need to remain properly informed of your legal obligations if such a case arises. At the very least, and confidentiality notwithstanding, you have to tell your superior (whether that is the president of your organisation, the senior youth worker or your line manger or employer) and you will have to decide together if further action is necessary. Of course, under such circumstances, you must keep the participant concerned fully informed and try to ensure that your action does not put them at any further risk.

General facilitation advice and information resources

Beyond the above considerations, you might find it useful to consider some general advice on facilitation of different kinds of youth work activity. An excellent exposé on how to facilitate human rights education activities can be found in COMPASS[4]. Further information on training in general can be found in the T-Kit 'Training Essentials'[5]. In addition, the following manuals created by other organisations are worth consulting if you are interested in familiarizing yourself with a variety of approaches to the facilitation of activities on gender and gender-based violence issues.

- "Shortcuts to Gender Equality: Methods and strategies regarding young people's leisure and associative activities", The Swedish National Board for Youth Affairs[6];
- "Empowering Young Women to Lead Change - A training manual", World Young Women's Christian Association[7];
- "Human Trafficking: Our Response – Manual for Peer Education", ASTRA[8];
- "Training Manual on Gender Based Violence", FEMNET[9].

In addition, the following manual produced by the International Women's Health Coalition (IWHC), entitled 'Positively Informed: Lesson Plans and Guidance for Sexuality Educators and Advocates'[10] has an excellent 'Additional Resources' section that is usefully organised according to different strands of educational work on gender related issues (for example, 'general sexuality education' or 'relationships'). This will be particularly helpful for additional background information on specific issues within the complex of gender issues one might address with young people.

---

4   www.coe.int/compass , pages 38 - 62
5   www.training-youth.net/INTEGRATION/TY/Publications/tkits/tkit6/index.html
6   www.ungdomsstyrelsen.se
7   www.ywca.org
8   www.astra.org.yu/en/pdf/istrazivanje6.pdf
9   www.femnet.or.ke/documents/gbv.pdf
10 www.iwhc.org/resources/positivelyinformed

4.4 List of activities

Title	Level	Group size	Time	Page
Expectations and demands	1	15-30	60 min	93
Gaining Status	1	6-30	60 min	95
Gender confusion	3	10-30	120 min	97
Gender-in-a-box	2	6-30	60-90 min	100
Good, Better, Best	2	8-14	60 min	106
Just once	2	6-30	90 min	110
Kati's story	4	10-20	60 min	114
Listen Closely	1	6-30	60 min	121
Media Bash	1	10-30	90 min	123
Safety in my life	2	8-20	60 min	126
Sex sells?	2	10-30	60-75 min	130
Spaces and Places	2	10-30	40-60 min	133
Stella	2	5-30	120 min	136
The Knight on the White Horse	3	10-20	60 min	139
Too hard to ask	3	6-30	60 min	143
What to do	2	6-30	60 min	147
General exercises for single sex groups				151

Expectations and demands[1]

"Nobody objects to a woman being a good writer or sculptor or geneticist if at the same time she manages to be a good wife, a good mother, good looking, good-tempered, well-groomed and non-aggressive." Leslie M. McIntyre

Complexity	Level 1
Group size	15 to 30
Time	60 minutes
Overview	This activity uses brainstorming techniques to help participants understand the different expectations towards and demands on girls/young women and boys/young men in contemporary society. It allows participants to explore concepts of gender further.
Objectives	To help participants distinguish between the differing expectations contemporary society puts on girls and boys, young men and young women
Materials	• Five sheets of flip chart paper • A big wall • Masking tape • A marker for each participant
Preparation	Hang five flipchart papers on the wall. Each one should be marked with one of the following typical settings in or from which girls / boys and young men / young women face expectations: • school • family • friends • society • partner Divide each flip chart into two columns; one column should have the title 'boys' or 'young men', and the other should have the title 'girls' or 'young women' on each.

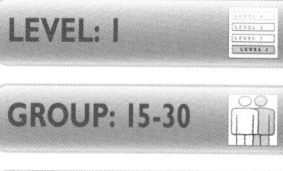

Instructions

Tell participants they should take a few minutes to think about what they believe is expected or demanded of girls and boys in the different settings identified on the posters on the wall. For this they can walk around or sit down and think, but they should do this part of the activity individually. Once they have ideas, they should write these down on the relevant part of the appropriate flip chart.

Once the brainstorming phase has been completed, divide the participants into five subgroups. Each group should select one of the flip charts and discuss its content.

---

1 Adapted from an exercise developed by "Intercultural Center, Foundation of Women's Forum, Sweden".

The following guiding questions may help participants in the discussion.
- What differences can you identify between the expectations and demands put on girls and boys?
- What would you like to change?
- How do you think it can be changed?

Each group reports the results of their discussion briefly to the whole group.

Debriefing and evaluation

Initiate the discussion by reviewing the results of the group work. Ask participants for their initial reactions to the results, how they feel about them, if anything surprised them and, if so, why.

Continue the discussion using the following guiding questions:
- Where do these expectations come from?
- Is it possible for boys and girls / young men and young women to fulfil these expectations?
- Who promotes these expectations?
- How do we ourselves promote them (whether consciously or unconsciously)?
- What are the effects of these expectations on young people?
- How can we / our organisations contribute positively to changing the situation?

Tips for facilitators

While this is a classic brainstorming and discussion activity, its theme, 'expectations on different genders', can be quite controversial. Expectations on different genders are also a matter of perception. As a result, this exercise can cause disagreement, as what for some participants may be perfectly reasonable expectations, for others may be overly demanding. The perception of expectations on different genders can also be linked to issues of values and socialisation. You can also focus the discussion on these related issues.

Suggestions for follow-up

Suggest that participants conduct longer-term observations of the expectations placed on different genders in real settings (for example, over one week or one month). The results of these observations could be compared to a survey of young people of different genders in the real settings (for example, school) about their perceptions of the expectations placed on different genders. You can initiate a discussion of the similarities and differences between the perceptions resulting from the survey and those resulting from individual observation.

Ideas for action

You can encourage members of your group to discuss what they would like to change in relation to this issue, and provide them with the opportunity and facilitation to prepare projects or actions to create change. Make sure that both boys and girls are involved in this process and find an equal voice for their ideas.

Gaining Status

"Many women do not recognize themselves as discriminated against; no better proof could be found of the totality of their conditioning." Kate Millet

Complexity	Level 1
Group size	6 to 30
Time	60 minutes
Overview	This is a brainstorming and prioritisation activity in which you ask participants to think about the status of girls in the society where they live, as well as broader questions of gender and gender equality.
Objectives	• To understand the status of girls in the contemporary society • To understand the social mechanisms by which society confers status on girls • To identify ways in which the status of girls can be improved
Materials	• Flipchart • Markers • Pens • Blank paper
Preparation	This activity does not require significant advance preparation but it is worthwhile for the facilitator to become acquainted with some factual information about the status of girls and young women in the society in which the participants you work with come from.

LEVEL: 1

GROUP: 6-30

TIME: 60 MIN.

Instructions

Ask participants the following question:
- What gives status to girls in your society?

You should take note of all the answers on a flip chart or wall chart. Brainstorm for as long as the ideas are flowing freely but for not more than 20 minutes or so. Then ask the group to split up into pairs and to rank the five most important things on the list from 1-5 (1 is most important, 5 is the least important). Give them 15 minutes to complete their ranking.

Then ask the pairs to compare their list with that of any other pair sitting close to them. Ask the groups of four to make their own rank order on the basis of the two lists prepared by the pairs. Give the groups 20 to 30 minutes for this ranking.

Ask the groups of four to present their rankings to the whole group.

Debriefing and evaluation

Begin the debriefing by reviewing the results of the ranking exercise. Is anyone surprised by any of the results? Ask participants if they consider anything particularly noteworthy?

- Is there any difference between the first list and the second list?
- Why do you think there is a difference?
- What do we want to change about the status of girls?
- What are we able to change?
- How can we change those things?
- Why are girls affected disproportionately when it comes to gender-based violence?
- What instruments are in place to protect the rights of girls?

Tips for facilitators

This exercise can also be well complemented by input and discussion on the European Convention on Human Rights and other human rights instruments, such as the Convention on the Rights of the Child. Consult COMPASS[2] for more information about these instruments of human rights protection or for good advice about working with ranking techniques if you have never worked with this method before.

Suggestions for follow-up

This exercise can be followed up appropriately by the development of group and personal action plans on the improvement of the status of girls.

Ideas for action

If participants demonstrate an interest in the issue of the status of young women and girls worldwide you can suggest that they consider reading more about it in the 'World Youth Reports' published periodically by the United Nations (Youth Unit). These can be found online at www.un.org/youth. Your group could, on the basis of the information gained, consider developing a campaign to improve the position and status of young women and girls locally or internationally.

---

[2] www.coe.int/compass

Gender Confusion

"Gender is not only male, female, man or woman. It is something much, much bigger. Gender is something that you define if you want to, not something that is to be forced upon you."

Complexity	Level 3
Group size	10 to 30
Time	120 minutes
Overview	This exercise is a combination of an analytical exploration of concepts used in the 'gender debate' and a critical and personal reflection on one's own gender. It also addresses sexuality and sexual orientation.
Objectives	• To make participants reflect upon their approach to gender as such and their own gender in particular
	• To demonstrate that gender is not only about women's issues and that it is not a static issue to be discussed along the dichotomy male-female or man-woman
	• To link issues of 'sexual orientation' with 'gender'.
Materials	• Pens and paper
	• Copies of your input for yourself and participants
	• Relevant visual aids or presentation equipment for the input
Preparation	Short input / presentation on terminology used in the gender debate covering terms such as sex, gender, man, male, woman, female, transgender, inter-gender. Definitions and explanations of these terms can be found in Chapter 1 of this manual.

Instructions

- Ask the participants to write down, individually, the first thing that comes into their minds when seeing the word 'gender'. Tell them to keep this piece of paper for themselves for a later stage in the activity.
- Introduce a brief presentation of the terminology commonly used in the gender debate covering terms such as sex, gender, man, male, woman, female, transgender, inter-gender. It is very important that you, as the facilitator, present a variety of definitions for each term to demonstrate that 'solid' and final definitions of these terms 'do not exist'. Rather, the definitions you present should be explained as 'possible definitions'. During the presentation and as each new term is introduced, encourage participants to engage in challenging and debating the definitions presented. If participants are not forthcoming by themselves, ask questions and invite them to express their opinion on what they have heard.
- Break the group up into smaller groups of maximum five people per group. Ask each group to spend a total of 20 minutes reflecting on what each of the concepts

presented means for the individual members of the group. The groups can be asked to discuss these on the basis of the following guiding questions:
- What feelings do I have when I encounter those terms?
- How do I see myself in relation to those concepts and the definitions presented for them?
- Do I agree with the definitions presented? Why / Why not?
- Can I identify with the any of the definitions for the terms presented? How / Why not?

The groups should prepare a short oral report that summarises the results of their discussion to be presented to the whole group in plenary.

- Bring the groups back into plenary and listen to the oral reports. Be sure to allow each group an equal amount of time and to ask if there are any questions of clarification needed after each of the reports. At this point issues that arise as a result of linguistic differences can also be addressed.
- Ask participants to write down, again, the first thing that comes into their head when seeing the word 'gender'. Ask them to look at the result of what they wrote the first time and to compare it to the new result.
- Initiate a debriefing discussion focusing on participants' reactions to any difference there may have been between what they wrote the first time and the second time in response to being asked to write down the first thing that comes to mind when seeing the word 'gender'.

Debriefing and evaluation

Ask participants to sit in a circle on the floor or on chairs. The following could be guiding questions for a debriefing discussion:
- Please share with the rest of the group what you wrote the first and second time you were asked to write down the first thing that comes to your mind when seeing the word 'gender'.
- Why do you think a difference emerged between the first and second response?
- Are you surprised by the difference if there was one? Why?
- Why do you think people have such different understandings of the terms relating to gender?
- How are those terms presented in the public sphere?
- How can language contribute to gender-based violence?
- Does gender related language and the way in which it is used contribute to discrimination?
- To what extent is there space for debating the definition of terms relating to gender where you live?
- To what extent do you think young people are involved in those debates?
- How can young people get involved in those debates?

Invite them to respond to the following process related questions:
- What did you learn during this activity?
- How did you feel during the activity?
- How do you feel now at the end of the activity?
- What have you gained from your participation in this activity?

Tips for facilitators

Be aware that the participants will have different approaches to and knowledge of the topic. Take into account that there may be confusion about the different terminology and linguistic differences, especially with regards to transgender issues. Try to explain and clarify without giving the impression that what you are telling the participants is 'the truth'.

Suggestions for follow-up

Think about inviting a guest speaker from a local LGBT or gender organisation to come and talk to the group further on gender and gender definitions. Participants can prepare questions before they come and the invited speaker can talk about what role gender definitions and common understandings of terms have within their organisation and the work that they do.

Ideas for action

If there are participants who demonstrate an interest in the more conceptual basis of issues relating to gender, you may suggest that they consider reading Chapter 1 of this manual.

HANDOUT

You may consider distributing copies of your brief input on the terminology and concepts related to the gender debate to participants after the input.

gender matters

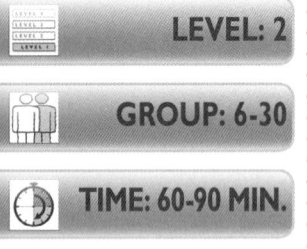

LEVEL: 2

GROUP: 6-30

TIME: 60-90 MIN.

Gender-in-a-box[3]

What are little boys made of? / "Snips and snails, and puppy dogs tails / That's what little boys are made of!" / What are little girls made of? / "Sugar and spice and all things nice / That's what little girls are made of!" 19th c. English rhyme

Complexity	Level 2
Group size	6 to 30
Time	60 to 90 minutes
Overview	Scholars and trainers alike often refer to 'gender roles'. This is a concept that is today relatively widely used and discussed in the public sphere. In communication, the existence of rigidly defined gender roles and the damage that these can cause to individuals is most often taken for granted. Nevertheless, participants may come from backgrounds where the difference between gender and sex is not acknowledged and where the different roles accorded to women and men are considered as something 'natural' or 'biological'. This exercise addresses the problematic effects of rigidly defined gender roles in society and aims to raise awareness about them. Participants will discuss the current role of the youth sector in this process and imagine possible change, as necessary.
Objectives	To help participants gain insight into • the socially-constructed nature of gender roles • the mechanisms and agents of gender socialisation • their personal history of gender socialisation • the connections between gender socialisation and gender-based violence
Materials	• Youth magazines • Advertising clippings • Flipchart with paper • Scissors • Glue sticks • Red, blue, green and black markers for the flipchart
Preparation	Prepare two flipchart posters. Each should have one of the following headings: MEN (written in blue) and WOMEN (written in red).

---

3 Adapted from Creighton, A. and Kivel, P. (1990). *Helping Teens Stop Violence. A practical guide for educators, counsellors and parents.* Hunter House, Alameda.

Instructions

The first part of this exercise can be conducted in sub-groups or in the whole group. You should decide about this in advance. If you decide to create sub-groups, examine whether it is more appropriate to conduct the first part of the exercise in single-sex sub-groups.

Refer to a common experience the group has had prior to this exercise, whether this was an introductory activity to this exercise or a movie they all know or pop-stars acting out extreme gender roles. Explain to participants that there is / was a strong message of gender socialisation in that experience, and that the following activity will be about examining gender socialisation in a very practical way.

When working with one large group

Form small groups of threes. Give out magazines or clippings and ask the small groups to leaf through them and discuss with each other the messages that young people receive from these magazines about what men and women are supposed to be like. While they are talking, prepare two empty flipchart papers on the wall or on two stands and write MEN in blue at the top of one of them and WOMEN in red at the top of the other. After about 15 minutes, ask participants to come back into one circle and to brainstorm on the qualities of 'real men' and 'real women' as presented through the magazines they have been looking at, and other sources where such images are present. Encourage participants to disclose examples of what they were taught to understand as a 'real man' or 'real woman' during childhood or in school. Make notes of qualities, preferably using key words or short phrases, on the two flipcharts, using the red and blue markers for women and men, respectively. In a multicultural or multiethnic group take note of differences that arise, including all the different gender roles that arise, for example, in some cultures thin women are considered more beautiful (usually places / groups where there is no food shortage), whereas in others (usually in places / groups where poverty and hunger are the norm) having more fat tissue is idealised as beautiful.

Once the lists are complete, ask the group to cut out a few image examples from the magazines and stick them next to the keywords listed on the flipcharts.

When using sub-groups

Form sub-groups. Present the magazines or clippings and the flipchart papers with MEN and WOMEN as headings. Introduce the exercise by asking the whole group to give a few examples about messages that young people receive about how 'real men' and 'real women' are supposed to be like from the video / role-play / experience they have in common. After receiving a few answers, explain that the group will now work in two sub-groups, one brainstorming on men, the other on women. If you have decided to use single-sex sub-groups, the male group works on the male roles and the female group should work on the female roles. They should look through the magazines and clippings and use them as illustrations wherever possible. Also tell participants that they should not limit themselves to what they have found in the magazines, but think of their own childhood, school years or adolescence and contribute with the messages they have received about what men and women should be like. Sub-groups should preferably work in separate locations. The facilitator should monitor the process.

When the sub-groups are ready, bring them back into one group, review the results and ask members of the other sub-group to add (some of) their own thoughts.

The result should look something like this:

MEN

faithful   (can be) polygamous   muscular   heterosexual
brave   sporty   father   had many girlfriends   hairy chest
strong   potent   creative   winner   rich   successful
daring   manager   protects the weak, esp. women   active
hits back   competent   breadwinner   intelligent   tall
clever   tough   does not show emotions (apart from anger)

WOMEN

(good) mother   pretty   married   sexy   monogamous
virgin(-like)   passive   (good) housekeeper   fertile   cheerful
has big breasts   long hair   graceful   takes care of her body
thin   less clever than boyfriend   no body hair   patient
sexually experienced   non-violent   keeps traditions   dresses well
obedient   family-orientated   silent   seductive   caretaker

Debriefing and evaluation

Explain to the group that despite some possible arguments on one word or another, very different groups of people usually manage to put together lists of these characteristics in a short period of time. Explain that the reason for this is that we all learn about how women and men should be from common sources. The collective name for these lists is 'gender roles'. These roles are presented to us as 'boxes' into which women and men are expected to fit. As you say this, draw a blue and a red rectangle around the words on the flipcharts.

Explain that what differentiates gender from sex is that, whereas the list of sexual characteristics is very short and has not changed in the last hundred thousand years, lists of gender roles are long, and vary both geographically and historically, often within a short distance or period of time.

Begin a discussion around the main issues raised by the exercise. You can use the following questions as a guide:

Gender socialisation
- Is it easy to stay in the boxes? Why?

Sometimes people do not *want* to stay in the box, but many times it is very difficult, or impossible to do otherwise.

Suggest to the group that they look for potential contradictions *within* the boxes, circle the pairs with green marker and connect them, for example:
- thin body - big breasts
- not hairy - long hair
- uses violence to resolve conflicts - kind to girlfriend

Some of these potential contradictions are biological: fat tissue on women does not (normally) grow only in one place; strong and long hair also means more hair on other body parts. Others expect different types of personalities in different situations.

Look for qualities that cannot be obtained by will, and box them in green, for example, physical qualities such as muscular, tall or thin are largely a matter of genetics and they can be influenced only to a certain degree. Becoming rich or being fertile are also qualities over which the individual has only limited influence.
- In what ways are we motivated to stay in, or try to get into the boxes?

Socialisation involves rewards and punishments as a way to reinforce or ban activities, habits and values. Ask participants to look at the contents of the boxes and to brainstorm how society punishes girls and boys, women and men, who do not want to or cannot belong to the box to which they are ascribed by society, in one respect or another.
- What is said to such people? What is done to them?

Note down the answers on a new sheet of flipchart headed 'Punishments' and list the brainstormed words in groupings for verbal, psychological, physical, sexual and social / economic forms of punishment. When the brainstorming is over, name the five forms of violence and give headings to the groups of words.

Conclude this part of the debriefing by explaining that these are some examples of the types of violence used to punish us and others, when we or they do not fit in. It is important to stress that there are many other causes and excuses for violence; the point of this exercise was to show the negative motivation which is responsible for so many of us actually trying to be who we are expected to be, but it is not an explanation of the causes of violence!

Gender roles and inequality between women and men

Gender roles equally limit men and women at the individual level. However, if we compare the two boxes, we find, first of all, that there are some important differences between them:
1. There are fewer contradictions in the male box.
2. Expressions in the male box often start with 'can be', whereas the women's box has much more of the obligatory type of qualities.

Furthermore, there are several opposites in the two boxes, which give more freedom and more power to men as a group, creating certain group privileges which are accessible to men as opposed to women, whether they ask for them or not.

Ask the group to find matching opposites in the men's and women's boxes, and then circle and connect them in black, for example:
- active - passive
- uses violence to resolve conflicts - non-violent
- earns well - family-centred

This exercise demonstrates that inherited gender roles and socialisation are partly responsible for the fact that men are encouraged to participate in the public sphere and in the political and economic life of the country. It is not surprising, therefore, that these systems are more representative of men's realities and needs. Women, on the other hand, are often encouraged to stay in the family sphere and to engage in care-taking, resulting in their disproportionate under-representation in decision making and their financial dependence on men. These severely limit the life options, choices and freedom of women.

Gender roles and gender-based violence

- Looking at the boxes now, what kind of connections do you think exist between gender socialisation and gender-based violence?
- Where do we learn the gender roles?

During the initial brainstorming and during the brainstorming on punishments, it is common for several sources to be raised. Make a new flipchart with the heading 'Sources of gender socialisation', and list the names of people and institutions that come up. Usually this list includes parents both before and after birth, kindergarten, school, peers, friends, the media (press, magazines, TV, commercials, music, movies, books, literature, science, fairy tales), religion, holy scripts, history books, popular psychology, the military, and so on.

Role and responsibility of the youth sector

- How does gender socialisation appear in the youth sector?
- Have there been or are there any changes in this field?
- Should the youth sector address this issue differently from current practices? If, yes then how?
- Can you give some examples of good practice?

Summary and conclusion

The existence of gender roles is often denied, with gender roles being considered 'natural'. How can something be natural and part of our biological set-up if it changes within ten years or a hundred kilometres? Here you can refer to cultural and geographical differences raised by participants during the brainstorming. Many individual boys and girls, women and men, suffer from the demands put on them to conform to specified gender roles. A rigid definition of gender roles contributes significantly to the inequality between women and men and to gender-based violence.

Tips for facilitators

The strength of this activity is that it brings the issue of gender roles and gender socialisation close to participants. Usually these issues are dealt with only in theoretical discussions. Therefore, it is important to introduce this exercise with some sort of real-life experience participants have. If you are working with a heterogeneous group coming together for a one-off training activity, it is best to create the experience right there in the room in the form of a role-play (e.g. boy and girl playing in a kindergarten or playground, and an adult instructing them to act like a boy and a girl), or a video showing boys and girls or women and men in typical or atypical gender roles, such as interviews with people having jobs that usually people of the other sex do. If the group meets often over a longer period of time, you can think of some recent or typical common experience, for example, that in camp, boys are usually called upon to look for wood and build the fire, whereas girls do the kitchen duties.

Suggestions for follow-up

Gender socialisation is part of almost every aspect of our life. The kind of examples that one finds in advertising or youth magazines can be found in many other areas of life, as well. As an add-on to the discussion on 'Where do we learn gender roles from?', the group could examine other sources of gender socialisation, such as first-grade schoolbooks, the policies and planned activities of their own organisation, and so on.

Ideas for action

The group can look for any pre-existing campaigns that address issues of gender socialisation and gender stereotyping and find ways to contribute to these campaigns through activities or creating publications or materials. Where the group can not find any pre-existing campaigns in which to take part in, they may like to think about how they can start their own campaign or produce information material to give to their organisation or other organisations.

Good, Better, Best[4]

"All is not what it seems"

Complexity	Level 2
Group size	8 to 14
Time	60 minutes
Overview	This activity illustrates gender stereotypes and the way society considers 'feminine' and 'masculine' characteristics desirable or undesirable.
Objectives	• To recognise that people are socialised to consider certain characteristics as feminine and others as masculine • To discover how society considers certain characteristics 'positive' or 'desirable', while other characteristics are considered 'negative' or 'undesirable' • To raise awareness of the almost automatic nature of social categorisation
Materials	• Two sets of cards with the different adjectives from the list below on them (see preparation and handouts) • A work and instruction sheet for each group
Preparation	Prepare the materials for the group work in advance

Instructions

Sets of cards

Each card has one part of a pair of adjectives written on it (see handouts). Although these pairs of adjectives form opposites, the stacks of cards should be sufficiently mixed so that it this not immediately very obvious.

Worksheets and instruction sheets

Worksheet for Group A

Prepare a blank sheet of paper divided into two columns. Each column should have a heading: one should read 'Feminine' and the other 'Masculine'. Prepare a separate sheet with the following instructions to add to the worksheet:

"Some characteristics are considered more feminine, while others are thought to be more masculine. Place the cards in the column where you think they belong. Work as quickly as you can, without thinking about it too much."

---

[4] Marietta Gargya, hotline worker at NANE Hotline for battered women and children, Hungary, developed on the basis of a research study by Broverman, I., Vogel, S. R. Broverman, D.M., Clarkson, F.E. and Rosenkrantz, P.S. (1972). 'Sex Role Stereotypes: A current appraisal'. *Journal of Social Issues,* 28. Blackwell. pp 59-78.

Worksheet for Group B

Prepare a blank sheet of paper divided into two columns. Each column should have a heading. One should read 'Positive / Desirable' and the other 'Negative / Undesirable'. Prepare a separate sheet with the following instructions to add to the worksheet:

"Some characteristics are considered more positive or desirable, while others are thought to be negative or not desirable. Place the cards in the column where you think they belong. Work as quickly as you can, without thinking about it too much."

See handouts for pre-prepared cards and work / instruction sheets

Explain that this exercise is about finding out how gender stereotypes work in society.

Form two groups with equal numbers of participants. Ask them to sit in two corners of the room. Hand out the envelopes with the cards and the worksheets with the instructions. Tell participants that they should follow the instructions on their worksheet and work as quickly as they can. Tell participants they have approximately 10 to 15 minutes to complete the task according to the instructions on the worksheet.

When ready, gather the whole group again. Write on the flipchart two headings: 'Feminine' and 'Masculine' and ask Group A to dictate the characteristics they put under the 'Feminine' heading. After each adjective, ask Group B if they placed that adjective in the Positive/Desirable or the Negative/Undesirable column. Note this information beside the adjective by putting a plus (+) or a minus (–) sign beside it.

Debriefing and evaluation

Ask for a round of first impressions about the exercise and its results. You can ask participants some of the following questions:
- How did you find the exercise? What did you like or dislike about it? Why?
- How do you feel about the results, now that you see the summary?
- Does anything about the results surprise you? What? Why is it surprising?

The following typical issues need to be addressed in the debriefing of the exercise:

a. Characteristics in the feminine column are likely to have minus (-) signs next to them, while the ones in the masculine column are likely to have plus (+) signs:
- What do you think about this difference?
- Where do these differences come from?
- Do you consider this characterisation of masculine and feminine attributes to be accurate or stereotypical?
- How do we learn gender stereotypes?
- Can you identify with any of them (in yourself or in people you know)?
- In your opinion, in what way do gender stereotypes affect the way we / other people evaluate or judge men and / or women?

b. The lists of men's and women's attributes (whether negative or positive) have a lot to do with our perception of men and women. These tend to inform the pre-conceived or ready made ideas we have when we meet people:

What do you think the consequences of gender stereotypes are on young women and men?
- What do you think can be done to deal with the negative consequences of gender stereotyping?
- How does gender stereotyping contribute to gender-based violence?
- How are people affected that don't fit into the gender stereotype?

Tips for facilitators

By way of introducing the conclusion to the debriefing, you may want to tell participants that research has found that children as young as 5 or 6 years of age have gender related stereotypes. It has also been found that consensus on the differences exist, regardless of age, education, sex or social status.

An additional dimension of the debriefing can focus on the fact that groups with undesirable characteristics are generally regarded as being less valuable and that they have lower status in society. This usually means that they are more often exposed to prejudice and to verbal or physical violence. You can ask participants to identify groups who are affected by such problems in their local area and ask how they think they can be overcome.

Suggestions for follow-up

Ask participants to think about ways to raise awareness about stereotypes and to prepare guidelines for how to go about confronting and challenging stereotyping in everyday situations. Ask them to experiment with following the guidelines in their everyday lives and to observe the results. Discuss their different experiences at a later meeting.

Ideas for action

Develop a 'research project' about stereotyping in everyday situations. If the members of your group attend school, discuss how they could observe and document stereotyping in school over a period of time. On the basis of the results, your group could propose recommendations to the school authorities for how to combat stereotyping, and the group could be involved in in-school activities to raise awareness about it among pupils.

HANDOUTS

Instructions for Group A

Headings: Feminine - Masculine

Some characteristics are considered more feminine, while others are thought to be more masculine. Place the cards in the column where you think they belong. Work as quickly as you can, without thinking about it too much.

Instruction for Group B

Headings: Positive/Desirable - Negative/Undesirable

Some characteristics are considered more positive or desirable, while others are thought to be negative or not desirable. Place the cards in the column where you think they belong. Work as quickly as you can, without thinking about it too much.

Set of Cards

dependent	independent
emotional	rational
objective	subjective
submissive	dominant
passive	active
skilled in business	not skilled in business
competent	incompetent
hesitates a lot	makes decisions quickly
ambitious	not ambitious
diplomatic	direct

gender matters

Just Once

"Men their rights and nothing more. Women their rights and nothing less."
Susan B. Anthony (1820 – 1906)

Complexity	Level 2
Group size	6 to 30
Time	90 minutes
Overview	This brainstorming and discussion activity aims to create a better understanding of the differences between arbitrary incidents of violence in a relationship and systematic abuse
Objectives	• To identify what constitutes violent incidents as distinct from abuse in a relationship • To discuss ways of recognising the difference between violent incidents and abuse in a relationship • To discuss differences in how to deal with violent incidents and abuse appropriately
Materials	• Flipchart • Markers

Preparation

Pre-prepare enough copies of the association pyramid (on flipcharts or A3 paper) for working groups as follows:

Draw a pyramid on the flipchart paper. 'Conflict' should appear at the top. You should draw two empty lines directly under it and a further two empty lines under each of those. You can extend the levels of association even further, but it is best not make the task too complicated. Three levels is usually enough to provoke a rich discussion.

Example:

Violent incidents

_____ _____

_____ _____ _____ _____

Instructions

Explain that in this exercise the group will discuss the differences and similarities between violent incidents between people in a relationship and an abusive relationship using the method of word association. The work of word association is best done in small groups, so if your group is bigger than six or so, form several small groups to work in parallel.

For the purposes of clarity, it can be useful to draw a big version of the association pyramid on a flip chart and show it to participants when explaining what the groups have to do. Explain that participants should fill in the association pyramid by thinking about the word at the top position of the pyramid (in our example 'Violent incidents') and writing the first two things they associate with it in the two empty positions immediately below. They proceed in the same manner for all the words through the levels of the pyramid.

For example:

Violent incidents

<u>Violence</u>   <u>Shouting</u>

_____   _____   _____   _____

The groups should prepare a second pyramid for the theme of 'Abuse'.

Explain that the participants of each group should decide together which words they consider most appropriate to associate with the word above through an open and mutual discussion of what they consider related to the main theme, and the words that are later added to the pyramid. Explain that everyone's ideas count and that everyone should feel their opinion is represented by the final result of the work of the group. The groups should be prepared to present the results of their work, including their flipcharts, to the plenary at the end.

NB: This part of the exercise can take up to 30 minutes, depending on how many people there are in each group and how many levels of the pyramid you ask them to fill in.

Finally, the groups present the results of their work to the plenary. Make sure that each group receives an equal amount of time for presentation, and remember to ask if there are any questions of clarification after each presentation.

Debriefing and evaluation

To initiate the discussion, refer directly to the outcomes of the group work. It is probably best to begin with a discussion of the first set of results (i.e. those for violent incident) and then proceed into a discussion of the results for abuse. The concluding part of the debriefing can link the issues.

Possible questions to guide the discussion:

On Conflict:
- Do you consider the descriptions of violent incidents in a relationship from the group work to be accurate? If so, why? If not, why not?
- Is there anything that has emerged in the exercise that you find surprising or which you were not aware of beforehand? Why / How?

- What about the final result at the bottom of the pyramids?
- Are there any contradictions between the results of the work of the different groups?
- Looking at the results of the group work, how would you define violent incidents in a relationship?
- What do you think causes violent incidents in a relationship?

You can use the same set of questions, with slight adaptations, to initiate a discussion on the results for 'abuse', for example:

- Looking at the results of the group work, how would you define an abusive relationship?

Already at this stage, different definitions for violent incidents and abuse will emerge. Try to keep track of the similarities and differences raised in the discussion. At this point, if there are items that appear in relation to both headings, point them out and discuss why they are characteristics of both conflict and abuse in relationships.

Having discussed what some of the differences between conflict and abuse in the context of relationships are, you can continue by discussing with participants what they consider to be appropriate approaches to dealing with each.

To conclude, ask participants about what they got out of the activity and how they feel they can follow it up:

- What do you feel you have learned from this activity?
- What do you think you (and your friends, group, organisation) can do to deal with the problem of abusive relationships?

Tips for facilitators

Word association activities depend to an extent on the language knowledge of participants, so be aware of the different levels of language competence in your group, especially if it is an international or multicultural group using one common language that is not their mother tongue. Furthermore, you are not necessarily fully aware of the kind of relationships participants are in or have experienced, so be careful not to ask direct questions about experiences of violent incidents or abuse. Additionally, be prepared for the possibility that a participant volunteers information of a personal and emotional nature about a previous or current experience of violent incidents and / or abuse.

Suggestions for follow-up

Contact a local organisation dealing with the issue of abuse in relationships and ask a representative of that organisation to come to meet the members of your group. Organise a discussion or a question and answer session about issues of interest to your group, for example, how to recognise an abusive relationship or how to provide support or help to a person trapped in an abusive relationship

Ideas for action

Initiate a research group with participants who are interested in finding out more about abuse in relationships. Encourage this group not only to search for 'theoretical' information about the causes of, responses to and legal provisions for prosecuting abuse, but also to contact organisations that are dealing with the effects of abuse and to meet former victims and perpetrators. Think about ways in which your group could support organisations or contribute to the promotion of their cause.

Kati's story

"I'm the one you love to hate."

Complexity	Level 4
Group size	10 to 20
Time	60 minutes
Overview	This activity strengthens empathy towards victims of interpersonal or relationship violence, and uses a symbol to raise awareness of the highly limited space and possibilities available to battered women. Furthermore, this activity demonstrates that leaving a violent relationship takes place in stages. Helpers will inevitably see only a small part of the development, which leads the person being abused to remove him- or herself from the violent situation.
Objectives	• To identify the stages of a typical battering relationship • To develop understanding for the lengthy process of leaving a violent relationship • To discuss the role of third persons (friends, family members, professional helpers, etc.) in helping a person remove him- or herself from a violent relationship
Materials	• An enclosed space large enough for your group to stand in a circle around a chair with doors that can be closed. • One chair for the middle of the room • Nine light blankets or bed sheets big enough to fully cover an adult

Preparation

Familiarise yourself with the issue of violence in relationships and battery before undertaking the facilitation of this exercise. Chapter 2 of this manual, especially the sections dealing with domestic violence and abuse, is particularly helpful in clarifying the differences in various kinds of violence. Refer also to COMPASS[5] pp. 354 to 357, for specific information on the human rights dimension of this issue.

Agree in your team, or with the other people who usually facilitate your group, who will be your co-facilitator. If you train alone, ask a participant to act as your co-facilitator. Check in the group if anyone has experienced this activity before. If so, ask one of these participants to act as co-facilitator. Go through the exercise with them in detail and explain their role to them. Make sure they understand what they are supposed to do and that they feel comfortable with it.

---

[5] www.coe.int/compass

In advance of the exercise, approach a participant you consider to be 'emotionally strong' and ask them whether they would agree to take on a difficult role in the exercise, that of Kati. Explain the entire exercise to them before they agree to take on the role. Make sure they understand the function of the blankets and what is going to happen to them. Make sure they do not suffer from any form of claustrophobia or anxiety.

Prepare the room by placing one chair in the middle and creating space so everyone can sit in a circle around it or in a semi-circle in front of it. Keep the blankets in a pile close to hand.

Instructions

- Introduce the exercise and its objectives. Explain that this activity's aim is to strengthen empathy towards victims of interpersonal or relationship violence, and that it uses a symbol to raise awareness of the highly limited space and possibilities available to battered women. Furthermore, this activity demonstrates that leaving a violent relationship takes place in stages. Helpers will inevitably see only a small part of the development, which leads the person being abused to removing him- or herself from the violent situation.
- Ask the participant that you have pre-selected and prepared to take on the role of Kati to come forward. Introduce the participant to the group. Tell the participants that s/he will have a difficult task, but s/he will be safe during the exercise. Tell the volunteer to sit on the chair in the middle of the room. Then introduce your co-facilitator to the group. Explain that this person will assist you in running the exercise.
- Pass around the blankets or sheets among participants evenly (1 for every 2 or 3 participants). The co-facilitator should get one.
- Explain to participants that you are going to read out a series of statements. There will be a short pause between each statement being read out. Participants should follow the text closely and especially pay attention to the pauses, as each of them will have a task to do during one or other of the pauses. Also tell them to pay attention to the co-facilitator, as during the first pause s/he will demonstrate what the participants will have to do later. To maintain the surprise effect, it is better not to tell the whole group straight away about the blankets. Explain to participants that the person playing 'Kati' has been briefed thoroughly, is fully aware of what is going to happen and has accepted the challenge.
- Ask participants to be absolutely silent during the active part of the exercise and tell them that if they have questions, they should keep them until the active part of the exercise has been completed. Tell them to take note of their feelings as the exercise goes on. If they have questions of clarification about how the exercise is supposed to proceed, ask them to raise them now, before the active part of the exercise begins.

- Start reading the story slowly. At the first pause, signal to the co-facilitator to put the first blanket over Kati. Make sure the co-facilitator knows in advance to cover Kati completely. Continue reading the next part of the story.
- At the next pause, encourage participants to put on another blanket. If participants are hesitant, you can look up, nod your head or signal to the co-facilitator to guide a participant in putting on another blanket.
- When you get to the part of the story where you ask Kati questions, read especially slowly. When you get to the first pause, signal to the co-facilitator to come forward to remove the first blanket. Again signal to participants that they should follow the example of the co-facilitator at the next pause. Usually participants do not hesitate to remove the blankets, but if they do, signal to the co-facilitator to guide them.
- After all blankets have been removed, thank the participant who played Kati, and ask her/him to sit back in the circle. Wait a moment before beginning the debriefing while participants settle themselves.

Debriefing and evaluation

Start the debriefing by asking for a round of impressions to get an idea of how everyone feels. This is quite an emotionally challenging exercise and participants may feel upset or uncomfortable. Remind participants that they have the right not to say anything. Offer the participant who played Kati the possibility to speak first about her feelings, and continue with others who indicate they want to speak.

During the debriefing, keep the paper with Kati's story at hand, so that you can refresh participants' memories of any particulars of the story, as necessary.

The following guiding questions can help you to develop the discussion:
- *How did it feel to put the blankets on Kati? How did it feel to watch others cover her? If you hesitated to cover Kati completely, why did you hesitate?*
- *How did you feel about the removal of the blankets?*
- *In your observation, how did other participants act during the covering and the removal? Were there differences?*
- *What do you think about the story? Can you identify with any of it?*
- *Who is responsible for Kati having been covered by so many blankets? Herself, her husband, or other people in the story?*
- *Why did we ask participants to cover and uncover her?*
- *Why were the blankets removed gradually? Why didn't we just remove them all at once?*
- *What do you think about the questions that Kati was asked when she was covered by nine blankets?*
- *In your opinion, what could be the different roles and responsibilities of the people in this story for ending the abuse?*
- *What is the responsibility of 'third parties', i.e. to individuals not belonging to either side?*

- *What is the responsibility of society?*
- *What do you think young people, youth workers and youth organisations can do to stop abuse?*

Tips for facilitators

This exercise needs a safe environment. It is not an exercise that can be run with a group that has only recently met. If your group works together regularly, this is an exercise for when they already know and trust each other and you (as facilitator). If your group has come together for a one-off residential activity, it is suggested that you run this activity only after the group has worked together for a few days. Participants having trust in the facilitator as well as in each other is crucial for the success of this exercise.

Make sure that no one makes any disturbances during the action. Avoid any coming and going in the room. If you run this exercise after a break or when somebody has left the room, make sure everybody is back in the room before you start.

It is up to you how you choose Kati, but it is strongly suggested that, prior to the exercise, you explain to the participant that s/he will be covered fully by several blankets. The volunteer must be claustrophobia-free and ready to experience some physical hardship during the exercise. You can also decide that a co-facilitator plays Kati. This is advisable if you have not, by this point, had the chance to build a high level of trust and safety in the group.

Some participants may hesitate at putting the blanket over Kati, or will prefer to put it on Kati's lap rather than over her head. The facilitator and co-facilitator should stay silent during the exercise, so try to encourage participants to perform the act of covering Kati fully by using eye contact and guidance. Bring into the debriefing stage any hesitations or unwillingness to perform, according to how the act of covering Kati is demonstrated.

Remember that you cannot necessarily know, as mentioned in the introduction to the exercises, 'who is in the room'. Someone may have experienced an abusive relationship and you should avoid causing such people to feel under pressure to disclose something they do not want to speak about with others or in public. Try to formulate the questions you ask in the debriefing in a 'non-personal' manner, so that even if they have personal experience, participants do not have to answer by referring to it directly.

Also be aware that such experiences may be painful for participants to be reminded of, and that as a facilitator it will be your responsibility to deal with the emotional consequences of running the exercise in your group. In other words, and in practical terms, if a participant gets upset or starts to cry, you have to be prepared to deal with that on a one to one basis and with the whole group. This may be as simple as taking a break, asking the participant if they want to go to their room to freshen up and telling the rest of the group that the person needed some time out and will speak about it when they are ready, or it may involve addressing the reasons for the participant getting so upset in the discussion in the whole group, with their prior consent, of course.

Variations on this exercise exist. You can alter the story to fit the environment you are working in. You can also make 6 to 8 steps rather than 9. Be sure, however, that you have an equal number of story steps for both the first phase and the second phase of the exercise (i.e. putting on and taking off blankets). Do not go above nine steps; staying under the blankets is no fun!

Suggestions for follow-up

It is possible to work with variations on this exercise by using a different 'story' to exemplify Kati's situation. You will find relevant case studies on the following website: www.nane.hu.

Check the Internet or local organisations that offer crisis intervention to battered women or other persons exposed to ongoing relational violence. Find out what support they give to victims. If possible, invite the representative of such an organisation to explain what they do to help in 'removing Kati's blankets'.

Have a look at the exercise 'Domestic Affairs' p. 114 to develop the theme of domestic violence and 'Power Station' p. 198 to develop the theme of how power and violence are related. Both exercises are from COMPASS[6].

Ideas for action

Consider providing information about domestic and relationship violence to your own target group. If you have not been active in the field of gender-based violence before, consult an NGO dealing with these issues for advice on how best to inform your target group about the problem, and raise their awareness as to how they can help themselves or others affected by it. Involve your group in the preparation of the information materials (e.g. flyers, blog, etc).

---

[6] www.coe.int/compass

MATERIAL

Kati's story

Kati is 28. She married Zoli when she was 20 and he was 23. They have two children, who are 3 and 7 years of age.

Co-facilitator covers "Kati" with first blanket.

When Kati was a child, she often saw her father beating her mother. It happened several times a week. Kati remembers that sometimes her mother had to go to the hospital because of her injuries.

Immediately after they get married, Zoli tells Kati that he will take care of the family income, because Kati does not know how to save. He tells her she will get from him only enough money to buy food and household items. He tells her she will have to show him receipts to prove that she spent the money on what she asked the money for and that he approved.

Kati gets pregnant in the first year of their marriage. Zoli starts to tell Kati regularly that she does not know how to run a household and that she is very lucky to have him, because nobody else would want her for a wife.

After the birth of their first child, Zoli starts to beat Kati. He accuses her of loving the child more than him.

Kati goes to her mother and tells her about being beaten by Zoli. Her mother tells her that this is part of marriage and she should learn to put up with it. According to her mother, "a woman has to stick with her husband".

As their first son grows older, Zoli threatens and beats him too. Kati is worried, but at the same time she believes that it can be very harmful to children to separate them from their fathers.

Kati tells one of her co-workers that she is regularly beaten by Zoli, and that she needs help. Her colleague tells the others at her workplace, and now everybody is talking about her.

Kati begins to miss more and more time from work without a proper excuse, so she gets fired. Now she does not have a job or an income of her own.

gender matters

(Question to the person in the middle and to mark the transition from covering to uncovering Kati)
Kati, why do you have to live like this? (Pause) Why don't you leave your husband? (Pause)

Kati reads a story in a magazine about a battered woman who manages to leave an abusive relationship. The article contains the phone numbers of hotlines, shelters, and drop-in centres for abused women.

Co-facilitator removes one blanket

Kati decides that she cannot bear being abused any longer. She called a hotline where she had a long discussion with a woman who told her that she is one of many women experiencing domestic violence.

For the first time Kati has an open discussion with her older son about their shared fear of their violent husband and father.

After a few weeks of thinking and planning, Kati calls her sister and asks her whether she could move to her place with her sons for a short period. Her sister had long given up hope that Kati would ever leave her violent husband and now she is very glad to be of help.

One afternoon Kati packs up their everyday belongings and moves with her sons to her sister's place.

She starts to look for a job. Her sister helps by asking friends if they know of any opportunities, and they look through the job advertisements together.

Kati visits a lawyer to get information about custody and child visitation issues and advice about how the truth about Zoli's violence towards them can be revealed. They also discuss divorce procedures.

Kati finds a job she likes, and moves into a rented apartment with her sons. She visits Child Welfare Services and finds out that her older son can enrol in a support group for children who have fled from violent homes.

Kati finds a self-help group of women who have survived domestic violence. Through sharing and listening she learns to understand how and why her romantic relationship developed into an abusive one. She decides that once she feels she is back on her feet, she will join a group to support battered women herself.

Listen Closely

"Nothing is ever said unless someone listens."

Complexity	Level 1
Group size	6 to 30
Time	60 minutes
Overview	Feelings of being ignored are common in discussions of gender. An exercise that focuses on communication can raise the problematic issue of exclusion based on gender.
Objectives	• To understand the process of exclusion based on gender • To understand the role communication can play in exclusion
Materials	None
Preparation	Make sure you are prepared to provide participants with examples of the kind of experiences or stories you have in mind. Prepare a large empty space in which the participant pairs can work without being distracted by each other.

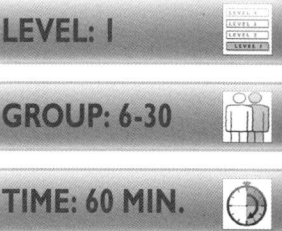

LEVEL: 1

GROUP: 6-30

TIME: 60 MIN.

Instructions

Ask participants to form pairs. One person is given the task to think of an experience or to tell a story. The other person should do everything to show that s/he is not listening, except speaking or walking away. After 2 to 3 minutes the pairs are asked to change roles and to repeat the exercise. When this is done the first person is asked to tell the same story again. This time, the listening partner should listen attentively and do everything to show that s/he <u>is</u> listening, even using small expressions or noises (e.g. "uh-huh".). Again, after 2 to 3 minutes, they swap roles.

Debriefing and evaluation

Begin with the process and how people felt doing the activity. The following questions may guide the discussion:
- How did it feel to be ignored?
- How did it feel to ignore someone?
- How did it feel to be listened to?
- How did it feel to be the attentive listener?
- Which role was best and why?

Continue with a discussion of the role that communication can play in processes of exclusion:
- What is meant by 'active listening'?
- How can you become an active listener?

- What can be gained from active listening?
- What can you do when you are being ignored?

Conclude by exploring how exclusion on the basis of gender works:
- What role does gender play in exclusion?
- How do the mechanisms of exclusion discussed affect young people in the context where you live?
- How can you or your organisation help young people overcome exclusion on the basis of gender?

Tips for facilitators

While this exercise is rather generic and can be used to explore communication and exclusion in relation to issues other than gender, it is important to remember that you are only using the exercise as a way into understanding processes of exclusion. Try, as far as possible, to draw out participants' own examples of exclusion based on gender in the debriefing discussion.

Suggestions for follow-up

Develop guidelines using brainstorming and discussion techniques for gender sensitive and inclusive communication with the participants which they can then apply in the settings where they meet exclusion based on gender. If you are interested in issues of social exclusion, we suggest you consult the T-kit on Social Inclusion http://www.training-youth.net/site/publications/tkits.

Ideas for action

Apply the gender sensitivity and inclusive communication guidelines in the group with whom you work. Ask the group to monitor their progress and evaluate the differences in their experience of the work within the group. Initiate a discussion in the local school and your organisation about mainstreaming such guidelines.

Media Bash

"Is no news good news?"

Complexity	Level 1
Group size	10 to 30
Time	90 minutes
Overview	This activity uses research and observation techniques to address the problematic use of violence in the media.
Objectives	• To 'confront' participants with the obvious use of violence in the media • To develop gender awareness among participants
Materials	• Flip chart • Magazines • Television • Computer • Computer games
Preparation	Make some space in the room (remove tables and chairs) so that the participants have space to work in groups on the preparation of a poster / flipchart.

Instructions

Inform participants that they are going to analyse TV programmes, read magazines, observe advertising and commercials, etc, using a pair of 'gender / violence glasses'.

If this activity is being conducted with a group that meets on a regular basis, tell participants that on this occasion the activity will be introduced and that they will have to watch TV and observe the media available in their local context during the upcoming week. This is a kind of homework task. In this case participants work alone and bring the results of their observations with them to the next session of the group.

Alternatively, if you are working in a in a one-off residential seminar, it is possible to run the activity on the spot, by conducting the analysis during the session on the basis of media materials chosen and provided by the facilitator. In this case the facilitator can also choose to record, in advance, relevant television programmes and advertisements as a supplement to print and other types of media. Participants may be asked to work alone or in sub-groups (depending on the number of people attending the seminar). In this case, and especially if participants are asked to work in groups, the facilitator should take into account that this kind of 'research and analysis' is a challenging task that is time consuming and should revise the time frame and the organisation of the discussion accordingly.

Whether working individually or in groups, participants are asked to:
- Count how many times they see violence or violent expressions in TV programmes, commercials, magazines
- Collect (cut out, record) expressions of violence as shown in media so that they may show them to the other participants
- Count how many times men are visualised as 'perpetrators' or as 'victims' of violence
- Count how many times women are visualised as 'perpetrators' or as 'victims' of violence
- Count how often they see a particular scene of violence from the point of view of the perpetrator or the victim
- Record the ways in which media encourage violence
- Record the extent to which media treat expressions of violence initiated by men and women differently

Ask participants to form groups of four and to share with each other what they found. Ask them to display the materials they collected (20 minutes). Then ask the entire group in plenary to compare the 'findings' and draw some conclusions on the use of violence and its impact for young people of different genders.

Participants will most probably find more 'male' expressions of violence. Discuss why violence committed by men is more frequently found in the media (and elsewhere?), as well as potential strategies for combating the kinds of violence referred to in the discussion.

Discuss violence against men and why it is such a sensitive and controversial issue.

Debriefing and evaluation

Ask participants if they have ever looked at the issue of violence through gender glasses before. If not, what did they learn by taking this new perspective? Did anything in particular surprise them?

More specifically, you can continue the discussion by asking the following guiding questions:
- What was the most 'eye opening' aspect of this activity?
- What did you learn from your participation?
- Are the materials found and displayed representative of where you live?
- How can the media be influenced to change the way it presents violence, stereotypical images of perpetrators of violence and different genders?

Suggestions for follow-up

Encourage participants and / or colleagues to undertake further reading or research into the issues of media and violence. Some relevant reading material in English includes the following books:
- Buckingham, D. (2000). After the Death of Childhood: Growing Up in the Age of

Electronic Media, Polity Press.
- Cohen, S. (2001). State of Denial: Knowing about Atrocities and Suffering, Polity Press.
- Shanahan, J. (1999). Television and its Viewers: Cultivation Theory and Research, Cambridge University Press.
- Kirsch, S.J. (2006). Children, Adolescents and Media Violence: A Critical Look at the Research, Sage.
- De Zangotita, T. (2005). Mediated: How the Media Shape Your World, Bloomsbury.

Some of the above are 'academic' books, in that they base themselves on research. Nevertheless, they are worth looking into for a better understanding of the relationship between violence, the media and society and as a backdrop to educational work in this field.

Run the activity 'Front Page', adapted to the issue of gender, with the same group for an in-depth exploration of bias and stereotyping in the media using simulative non-formal education techniques, p. 135, COMPASS[7].

Ideas for action

Contact your local media providers and ask them about their policy on the reporting of violence. Challenge them to use 'gender lenses' in developing their approach to reporting violence. Organise a discussion in your group with media professionals and students about the responsibility of media professionals for the contents and approach of their reporting.

---

7 www.coe.int/compass

Safety in my life[8]

"It is hard to fight an enemy that has outposts in your head." Sally Kempton

Complexity	Level 2
Group size	8 to 20
Time	60 minutes
Overview	This activity illustrates gender differences related to the issue of violence, and addresses the lack of availability of appropriate information for young people on the true nature of interpersonal violence such as relationship violence or bullying, etc.
Objectives	• To recognise the different levels and areas of concern for safety that men and women, and boys and girls have • To discover the gap between the realities of gender-based violence and the information young people receive • To identify some ways in which youth work can play a role in filling this gap
Materials	• One flipchart sheet and markers for each of the sub-groups
Preparation	Set out a circle of chairs in the middle of a large free space for the introduction to the activity Place flip chart paper and markers in different places in the room or space, close to where the groups will work be working

Instructions

Explain that this exercise is about bringing together what individuals regularly do in order to be and stay safe. Tell participants that single sex groups will create lists of their own, and then will share them and discuss their findings together.

Form sub-groups. These should be single-sex groups, each of a maximum of four or five people. Tell the groups that they should share and brainstorm on the subject of 'staying safe', in other words, participants should think about and share things they actually do to avoid violence and to stay safe from violence. They should also think about the kind of threats to their safety they actually face on a regular basis.

Ask each group to go to the prepared working spaces in the room or close by. Give the groups about 20 minutes for the reflection and to make a list on the flip chart.

Get the groups back together, and ask each to report. Hang all the flipcharts next to each other in a visible place. If there were several sub-groups of the same sex, place those flip-charts next to each other.

---

8   Adapted from Adams, M., Bell, L.A. and Griffin, P. (Eds.) (1997). *Teaching for Diversity and Social Justice*. Routledge, p. 122.

Debriefing and evaluation

Ask for a round of first impressions about the exercise and about the results. A good way to kick off this discussion is to check if anyone is surprised by the discussion they had in the group, or by the results of their or other groups' work.

Typical results that arise and need to be addressed include:

The lists prepared by the women's group/s are often far more detailed and longer than that of the men's group/s and cover more types of threat to women's safety:
- What do you think about this difference?
- Where do you think it comes from?
- Does socialisation play a role?

The lists prepared by both male and female groups often focus heavily on precautions against violence from complete strangers, even though there is evidence that violence is most often perpetrated by people known to victims:
- Are the lists of threats representative of the actual dangers boys and girls, men and women face in their daily lives? Why? Why not?
- If not, what dangers are missing from the list?
- Why do you think they did not appear in the discussion and are therefore missing?
- Can you identify any of the dangers in your local context? If so, do you think the precautions for staying safe suggested by the groups are relevant or effective?

You can continue the debriefing by initiating a discussion about the information that young people receive about violence:
- What kind of information do we receive about violence and safety from violence? Where does such information come from? Is it credible? Do young people take it seriously?
- Why do you think children and young people are warned about certain dangers or forms of violence, but not about others?
- Whose job is it or should it be to inform young people and children about violence and precautions for staying safe?
- In what way could the youth sector contribute to providing credible information and advice to young people about violence and staying safe?
- How could you or your organisation contribute to making a change in this respect?

Tips for facilitators

This exercise requires a certain level of consciousness from the group regarding what violence is, what forms of violence exist and how they are defined. Make sure you read the information about violence in Chapter 2 of this manual in preparation for running the activity, so that you can help participants clarify any confusion that may exist around the different types of violence that can be observed in everyday life. You can also read COMPASS pp. 376 to 381 for a summary of different ways of understanding violence.

Be aware that if most participants have the attitude that they are safe from violence, an attitude that often results in victim blaming, this exercise can raise 'prejudiced' attitudes towards victims of violence. When talking about taking precautions against violence or being active in the defence of one's own safety, the balance in the discussion can easily tip in the direction of placing blame on the victims for not having done enough for themselves. Make sure that both direct and meta-communication makes clear that perpetrators are always responsible for their own actions. A lack of information about safety or being in a vulnerable position for objective or subjective reasons does not cause violence and people not ensuring their own safety do not decide to become victims. Perpetrators, on the other hand, actively decide to use violence.

Explain that violence is a social phenomenon, as opposed to aggression, which is a biological one. As such, being safe from violence requires learned social skills. Make sure you focus the discussion on the extent to which society, through its different institutions from family to school, prepares young people for the most typical forms of violence committed against them.

Suggestions for follow-up

If anyone is interested in further reading, the recent publication 'Young People and Violence Prevention – Youth Policy Recommendations', edited by Gavan Titley and published by the Directorate of Youth and Sport, provides an easy-to-understand guide to the issue of violence in the everyday lives of young people, and some insights into how to combat it. This book is available for downloading on http://book.coe.int/youth.

Organise a discussion activity around the data on crime and violence provided by national statistical offices, for example, the British Crime Survey Data or the U.S. Bureau of Statistics data, on violence and perceptions of safety among young people or among women and men. Two examples of the kind of data that can be used to initiate a discussion activity are provided below.

Question: "How safe do you feel walking alone in this area after dark?"[9]

		% Feeling 'Very Unsafe'	% Victims of Street Crime
Men:	16-30	1	7.7
	31-60	4	1.6
	61+	7	0.6
Women:	16-30	16	2.8
	31-60	35	1.4
	61+	37	1.2

Bureau of Justice Special Report: 'Intimate Partner Violence, May 2001' from www.coolnurse.com, accessed on April 24, 2005.

---

9 Hough, M. and Mayhew, P. (1983). The British Crime Survey: first report. Home Office research study No. 76. London: HMSO. p. 25. Fears for Personal Safety After Dark and Risks of 'Street Crime'

"A survey of adolescent and college students revealed that date rape accounted for 67 percent of sexual assaults. More than half of young women raped (68 percent) knew their rapist either as a boyfriend, friend or casual acquaintance. Six out of ten rapes of young women occur in their own home or a friend or relative's home, not in a dark alley".

Run the activity 'Violence in my life', p. 248 in COMPASS, www.coe.int/compass with the same group in order to exemplify experiences of interpersonal violence (in general, not just gender-based).

Ideas for action

Suggest to the group that they research into programmes that exist in the local area which do violence prevention with young people, and that they get in touch to find out more about what they do and how. Discuss with your group how you could collectively contribute to violence prevention efforts.

Suggest to the group that they review school programmes to see the extent to which they address these issues as part of the curriculum. If there is an obvious lack of and need for violence prevention programmes in a given school, suggest that the group considers developing a project in cooperation with a specialised organisation to initiate a violence prevention or human rights education programme with a gender focus in the school.

gender matters

Sex sells?

"Does it make the difference?"

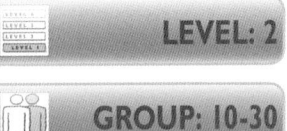

Complexity	Level 2
Group size	10 to 30
Time	60 to 75 minutes
Overview	This exercise addresses a number of issues, including relations between different genders, advertising presentations of males and females, perceptions of what is male and female in advertising and the influence of advertising on the creation of public perceptions regarding gender, sex and sexuality.
Objectives	• To identify everyday presentations of gender using the example of advertising in the media • To identify gender stereotypes projected through the media • To reflect upon and discuss the social construction of gender roles • To raise awareness about inequality of opportunity between genders • To promote empathy with the other gender
Materials	• Newspapers and magazines • Scissors • Glue • Flipchart paper
Preparation	Collect various different newspapers and magazines, rich in advertisements and pictures in both colour and black and white. Read the instructions carefully and study the grid that participants will use in the second part of the exercise (see handouts).

Instructions

- Introduce the activity. Start by referring to everyday life and common perceptions of different gender roles in society. Explain that it is almost impossible to find dimensions in life where the aspect of gender is not present. Even when we think of basic things, such as who will wash the dishes at home, the seating arrangements of girls and boys in schools, places where women and men are employed, gender is present. Explain that advertisements in the media very often benefit from the different characteristics, stereotypes and prejudices that are current in a society about genders.
- Tell participants to look through the supplied newspapers and magazines and choose one advertisement to analyse.

- Using the grid (see handouts), each participant should then identify and note down the different parties in the advertisement, the direct (obvious) and any possible hidden messages that it conveys and the use made by the advertisement of gender stereotypes.
- In addition to the grid, ask them to write down the attributes of men they find in the advertisement on blue post-its, and the attributes of women they find in the advertisement on pink ones.
- Once participants have filled out the grid (give them about 20 minutes for this task, to include time for reflection), ask them to get together in pairs to share with each other the advertisements they chose, the grid they prepared and their gender analysis (blue and pink post-its with attributes of men and women). (Give the participants about 20 minutes for this task as both participants in the pair need time to present and share.)
- When participants finish the work in pairs, the facilitator should collect the blue and pink post-its prepared by the individual participants and present them to the plenary, putting each colour post it on separate flip chart (one for women's attributes and one for men's), reading out the words on the post-its.

Debriefing and evaluation

Ask participants to comment on the attributes given to men and women. They may also make reference to the advertisements, but it is not necessary to receive complete oral reporting from the pairs.

Some questions you can put to the group to initiate a discussion on this issue include:
- How do you feel about the male and female attributes identified as a result of the analysis of the advertisements?
- In your opinion, are these attributes accurate for men and women you know, or in general? How / how not?
- To what extent do you consider such portrayals appropriate, and why?
- How are these attributes reflected in the context where you live?
- Where do you come across such presentations of male and female attributes?
- What do you consider to be the consequences of such portrayals of women's and men's characteristics?
- In what way do such portrayals of women's and men's attributes in advertising affect the perception and self-perceptions of young women and men?
- How do you think advertising can avoid the use of stereotyped and negative portrayals of women and men?
- In what way can advertising contribute to forms of gender-based violence?
- Can advertising contribute to violating people's rights? How?
- How can you / your organisation contribute to the creation of more gender equitable advertising practices?

gender matters

Tips for facilitators

Be aware that advertising often uses overtly sexual images or covert sexual messages about women or men to 'sell' the product they are advertising. This aspect certainly has to be addressed by a discussion of this nature, but remain aware that discussions that have content relating to sex may cause discomfort to some participants.

Suggestions for follow-up

Ask the group to develop a code of ethics for media professionals working in the areas of advertising and marketing concerning the presentation of gender in the media. Use prioritisation or ranking methods.

Ideas for action

Contact local media professionals, especially working in the area of marketing and advertising, to discuss the issue of the presentation of gender in the media. If your group has already worked out a code of ethics, ask the media professionals to comment. Alternatively, invite media professionals to come to meet the members of your group and organise a panel discussion on the issue of the presentation of gender in the media. Consider inviting feminist activists with strong views on the issue to take a key role in the discussion.

HANDOUT

Grid for Analysis

	What?	Who?	(In-)Appropriate?	Why?
Role				
Behaviour				
Activity				
Attribute				

Spaces and Places

"How safe is safe…?"

Complexity	Level 2
Group size	10 to 30
Time	40 to 60 minutes
Overview	This exercise explores the safety of Lesbian, Gay, Bisexual or Transgender (LGBT) young people in different 'everyday' situations and locations.
Objectives	To raise participants' awareness of the fact that openly Lesbian, Gay, Bisexual or Transgender young people may feel unsafe when entering (public) spaces
Materials	• A large empty wall-space along which there is space for the participants to move • Three large pieces of paper of three different colours with the titles 'VERY SAFE', 'UNSURE' and 'VERY UNSAFE' written on them
Preparation	Prepare three separate large pieces of paper of three different colours with the titles 'VERY SAFE', 'UNSURE' and 'VERY UNSAFE' written on them. Hang the posters on a large empty wall along which there is space for the participants to move in each direction. Leave a large space between each of the posters on the wall. The poster with 'UNSURE' written on it should be placed in the middle of the other two.

Instructions

Ask participants to imagine the room is a giant opinion scale with one end of the room representing 'very safe', the middle 'unsure', and the other end 'very unsafe' on the scale.

Ask participants to think about how safe they imagine it is for LGBTs to be 'out' (i.e. open about their sexuality) in a variety of settings:

- at a gay or lesbian bar
- during a classroom discussion at school
- during a pop concert where homophobic slogans are chanted by the singers
- in a conversation with parents
- during a discussion at school where racist, homophobic and xenophobic remarks are made
- at a gay or lesbian bookstore

- at the work place
- in a local youth club in a highly culturally diverse urban area
- asking for condoms at a village pharmacy
- at a youth conference or training course where, despite good intentions from the organisers, homophobic remarks are expressed by participants

To clarify the differences of opinion in the group, and to create a basis for discussion, ask participants to move to the place on the scale at which they feel the setting raised corresponds. Some will move to the part of the room corresponding to 'very unsafe'. Others will move to less extreme positions on the scale.

At this point ask participants to justify the position they have taken by asking why individual participants think a particular setting is more of less safe for LGBTs who are 'out'. You have the choice at this point to encourage participants to discuss in more or less depth about their different perceptions. Try to ensure that participants speak from positions of experience or provide relevant, evidence-based arguments for their positions. Participants should speak for themselves rather than arguing why they think others are wrong, although making references to other people's arguments is perfectly acceptable. Repeat the procedure for several or all the settings on the list. Decide in advance how long you want to devote to the discussion in each round (5 minutes? 10 minutes?). This will inform you how long you need for the overall exercise.

Debriefing and evaluation

This exercise can be debriefed in more or less depth and with a variety of focus issues. Depending on the group you are working with (its composition and size), on the time you have available and on what you want to achieve by running this activity, you can choose what emphasis to give the debriefing.

Here, we outline a debriefing that charts the middle ground, offering several related directions in which the discussion can be led.

Ask participants to sit in a circle. Get a round of first impressions about the exercise and about the results. A good way to start this discussion is to check if anyone is surprised by the opinions demonstrated by the exercise.

You can continue the discussion by focusing on the differences in perceptions and asking, for example,

- Why do you think there are differences in perception concerning the safety of different everyday places for LGBTs who are 'out'?
- Based on the results of this exercise, what do you consider to be the characteristics of settings which can be considered as 'unsafe' for LGBTs?
- Based on the results of this exercise, what do you consider to be the characteristics of settings which can be considered as 'safe' for LGBTs?

- Can you identify any of the situations of relative safety or lack of safety described in this exercise in your local context?
- What dangers do young LGBTs who are 'out' face in your local context?
- What do you think that responsible players in each of these settings can do to help LGBTs who are 'out' to feel safe?
- What precautions can young LGBTs take to increase their own safety?

You may broaden the discussion to take into account the ethnic, religious and cultural differences within the LGBT movement. For example, would a transgender man or a black lesbian woman be more vulnerable to intolerant and violent behaviour? What do racism and trans-phobia mean for the safety of LGBT people?

This can, for example, open up a wider discussion on the problem of vulnerability to gender-based violence. You can ask participants to think about how safe female representatives of (visible) minority groups might feel when entering settings usually dominated by male members of the majority.

Tips for facilitators

The list of settings given here is not exhaustive. You might consider revising the list to make a strong link with the context and reality of participants.

It can be useful for the debriefing that the facilitator or a co-facilitator notes down the results for each setting in a place visible for the participants, in other words, how many people thought the setting discussed was unsafe or safe, etc. It can also be very useful to note down some of the arguments used by participants for later reference, if you decide to go into a deeper discussion.

Suggestions for follow-up

Run the activity 'Where do you stand?' using statements adapted to the themes of gender and gender-based violence, Compass[10], pp. 254.

Ideas for action

Suggest that your co-activists in your organisation or your group conduct an 'inclusivity analysis' of your organisation. This can be simply done by reviewing organisational policies and practices to check whether or not they are safe, welcoming and open to LGBT young people, although it does require a large measure of openness to self-critique on your part and that of the others in your organisation. Alternatively you can use a more sophisticated or scientific method. Several of these exist in the youth gender field and can be found by searching the Internet.

---

10 www.coe.int/compass

gender matters

Stella[11]

"In a sad love story, who's the worst and who's the best?"

LEVEL: 2

GROUP: 5-30

TIME: 120 MIN.

Complexity	Level 2
Group size	5 to 30
Time	120 minutes
Overview	This activity uses ranking techniques to confront the differing values of participants in relation to issues of morality, and to open up discussion on the issues of gender inequality and socialisation into gender-based stereotyping and prescribed gender roles for both women and men
Objectives	• To encourage participants to think about their own values in relation to morality and gender • To analyse where differing moral positions come from • To understand how individuals become socialised into gender-based stereotyping or prescribed gender roles • To analyse the way prescribed gender roles for both women and men are an intrinsic part of individual and societal morality
Materials	1 copy of Stella's story for each participant
Preparation	Enough space for participants to work individually, in small groups of 3 to 6 and in plenary.

Instructions

Introduce the exercise to the participants. Explain its objectives and that it will help participants to find out more about their personal values in relation to morality and gender.

Ask participants to read the story individually and to rank each character (Stella, Vitali, Ralf, Stella's mother and Goran) according to their behaviour, for example, "Who acted in the worst way?" "Who was the second worst?", and so on. You should give participants 10 minutes for this task.

When everyone is ready with their individual ranking, ask participants to get together in small groups (of 3 to 6), to discuss how they perceive the behaviour of the characters. The task of the small groups is to come up with a common ranking – a list that everybody in the small group can agree on.

Ask them to avoid using mathematical methods in order to establish the ranking, but rather to build the list on the basis of a shared understanding and agreement about what is good and what is bad behaviour.

---

11 Adapted from "Abigale" Training Resource File Volume 4 – "Intercultural Learning" Examples of Methods Used, Directorate of Youth and Sport, Council of Europe – CEJ/G (1991) 4 rev.

After the small groups have come up with their lists, you can optionally repeat this phase by bringing two small groups together to form medium size groups. If you choose to include this phase, the first round of group work should be conducted in groups not larger than 4 people.

Debriefing and evaluation

Start by bringing together the results of the group work and by discussing the similarities and differences between them. Slowly move on to ask on what basis people made their ranking. You can use the following questions to guide the discussion:
- How did they decide, individually, what was good and what was bad behaviour?
- How did they find agreement in the small groups about what was good and bad behaviour?
- Did they find it difficult to come to an agreement that everyone could live with?
- What obstacles were encountered?
- What role do personal values play in such a process?
- Where do one's personal values, in relation to issues of morality and gender, come from?
- Where do people learn morality and gender related values?
- Can you identify any prescribed gender roles in the story?
- What gender related dilemmas are raised by this story?
- Are any of these present in the context where you live?
- How do these issues affect young people?
- How can we help young people to deal with social pressure related to morality and gender?

Tips for facilitators

In order to get the best results from the exercise, it is essential that you establish an open atmosphere in which every ranking of the story is explicitly acceptable, and where you do not start 'blaming' people for arguments you might consider strange or bad yourself.

Suggestions for follow-up

This exercise can be adapted in many ways. One variation is to run it as done here, and then to repeat it with a changed story, in which all the women become men, and vice-versa. Does the same ranking still apply? Why do things change? You could also include the age of the characters in the story and play around with it, make them all have the same gender, or include ethnic or national background. It would then be useful to look at how the changes in the story make a difference to the ranking, and why.

Ideas for action

Suggest to your group that they explore the issue of values as they relate to gender in a variety of real communities. You can do this in a number of ways: develop a series of interviews using different audio visual methods with male and female representatives of different religious and cultural communities, or invite women and men from the communities you are interested in knowing more about to come to meet the members of your group and to discuss values related to gender.

HANDOUT

Stella's Story

Somewhere, far, far away, lives a beautiful girl Stella. She loves handsome Vitali who lives on the other side of the river. In early spring a terrible flood destroyed all the bridges across the river, and has left only one boat afloat. Stella asks Ralf, the owner of the boat, to take her to the other side. Ralf agrees, but with one pre-condition: he insists that Stella sleep with him. Stella is confused. She does not know what to do and runs to her mother to ask for advice. Her mother tells her that she does not want to interfere with Stella's private business. In desperation Stella sleeps with Ralf who, afterwards, takes her across the river. Stella runs to Vitali to embrace him happily, and tells him everything that has happened. Vitali pushes her away roughly and Stella runs away, bursting into tears. Not far from Vitali's house, Stella meets Goran, Vitali's best friend. She tells him everything that has happened. Goran hits Vitali for what he has done to Stella and walks away with her…

The knight on the white horse[12]

"If you think you are too small to have an impact, try going to bed with a mosquito in the room." Anita Roddick

Complexity Level 3

Group size 10 to 20

Time 60 minutes

Overview This activity introduces the difficulties of recognising abuse from close up and early warning signs for who could be a potential abuser. It is a good basis for a discussion on how society romanticises violence and oppression.

Objectives
- To discuss the boundaries of a safe and democratic relationship
- To discuss the role of education and / or youth work in preventing violence in intimate relationships

Materials Copies of the story of the knight on a white horse for Susie, the narrator and the knight

Preparation

Familiarise yourself with the issue of violence in relationships and battery before undertaking the facilitation of this exercise. Chapter 2 of this manual, especially the sections dealing with domestic violence and abuse, is particularly helpful for clarifying the differences in various kinds of gender-based violence. Refer also to COMPASS[13] pp. 354 to 357 for specific information on the human rights dimension of this issue.

Choose two participants or team members with whose help you feel confident to co-facilitate this exercise. Brief them in advance about what will happen during the activity. Give them a copy of the explanation of the exercise to read in advance and a copy of the story of the Knight on the white horse. If possible, the person that plays Susie (and is 'courted') should be female. If you do not think that any participant is suited to the role, ask a (female) team member to be Susie. The other participant or team member should be the narrator. You (the facilitator) play the knight.

Prepare the working space so that all participants can sit in front of the actors in a semi circle and can observe all the action clearly.

> Don't forget to read the tips for facilitators before running this activity.

---

12 Adapted from an activity elaborated by NANE Women's Rights Association, Hungary http://www.nane.hu
13 www.coe.int/compass

Instructions

Explain to participants that they will hear a short story about the knight on the white horse and that afterwards there will be a discussion about the feelings it raises.

The actors move to the middle of the room. You (the facilitator) are the knight. You kneel in front of Susie, or sit next to her, and hold her hand. It is preferable for you to act out the 'courting' scenes by heart, rather than reading. So, if possible, learn the dialogue by heart in advance. The narrator stands to the side of the scene. The narrator reads out their part of the story.

The text of the story is outlined in the handouts section below.

Debriefing and evaluation

After the 'courting scene' and story have been completed, check the faces of participants for reactions or emotions. If participants seem a little shocked or upset, give the participants a very short break for them to collect themselves together.

Begin the debriefing by asking the person who played Susie to share her feelings and impressions about the little play before collecting the impressions of the other members of the group. Keep the story in your hands for reference and remind the group of certain passages of the story as necessary.

You can initiate the discussion using the following questions as a guide:
- What does this story make you feel? Why?
- What do you think about this relationship?
- At which point do you think Susie should have realised this is a dangerous relationship?
- What other signals are there that indicate that this relationship is becoming abusive?
- What can we understand about romantic relationships from this story?
- Where does an open and democratic relationship end and an abusive one begin?
- Where do we get our knowledge about what relationships should be like from? How accurate are these sources of knowledge?

You can conclude the discussion by widening the focus to include how society romanticises violence and oppression. You can use the following questions to guide this part of the discussion.
- Where and under what circumstances do we most often come across violence and gender-based violence in particular?
- In what way is violence and / or gender-based violence depicted?
- To what extent is violence romanticised?
- How do young people engage with these images or depictions of violence?
- How does this affect the way young people develop their capacity for relating to other people and especially to members of another gender or people with a different sexuality?

- What can be done to ensure that gender-based violence is portrayed more honestly and realistically?

Tips for facilitators

This exercise can be very emotional for some participants and, therefore, needs a safe environment. This is not an exercise that can be run with a group that has just recently met. If your group works together regularly, this is an exercise for when they already know and trust each other and you (as facilitator). If your group has come together for a one-off residential activity, it is suggested that you run this activity only after the group has worked together for a few days. Participant trust in the facilitator as well as in each other is crucial for the success of this exercise.

As mentioned previously, bear in mind that you do not necessarily know 'who is in the room'. Someone may have experienced an abusive relationship and you should avoid such people possibly feeling under pressure to disclose something they do not want to speak about with others, or in public. Try to formulate the questions you ask in the debriefing in a 'non-personal' manner, so that even if they have a personal experience, participants do not have to answer by referring to it directly.

Also be aware that such experiences may be painful for participants to be reminded of, and that as a facilitator it will be your responsibility to deal with the emotional consequences of running the exercise in your group. In other words, and in practical terms, if a participant gets upset or starts to cry, you have to be prepared to deal with that on a one to one basis and in the whole group. This may be as simple as taking a break, asking the participant if they want to go to their room to freshen up and telling the rest of the group that the person needed some time out and will speak about it when they are ready, or it may involve addressing the reasons for the participant getting so upset in the discussion in the whole group, with their prior consent, of course.

Suggestions for follow-up

See the activity 'Kati's story' (see p. 110) and explore it with same group to develop the theme of domestic violence and abuse.

Ideas for action

Participants can get in touch with a local hotline for women experiencing trouble in their relationship and domestic violence. They can help find ways to advertise the hotline to the general public and some may even wish to become a volunteer for the hotline. If there are no such local hotlines, participants may want to look further into finding a way to establish one for the local community. It is important to note that when working for a hotline or establishing a hotline, it is extremely important to undergo training to be able to respond to the calls effectively.

HANDOUT

The knight on a white horse

Knight	Wow Susie! You are so beautiful! I love your style so much! You are such an individual, and I love that about you…!
Narrator	… and Susie is very happy and feels very attracted to the man
Knight	I've never felt so close to anyone. You are the only one I trust, the only one I can share my problems with and who understands them. It is so good to be with you. I love you so much…
Narrator	Susie feels that she is very important to the man. She feels safe.
Knight	I feel I have found my other half. We have been created for each other. We don't need anybody else, do we?
Narrator	And Susie indeed feels that the whole world is left outside, and that every minute they spend away from each other shortens their love.
Knight	You are so beautiful, so pretty. But don't you think that your skirt is a bit daring? Don't you understand, I'm just worried about you! I think you should wear something else. That would make me feel better. We belong together, don't we? You are mine.
Narrator	And because Susie loves him, and would not want an argument for such an insignificant thing, she changes the way she dresses to suit his wishes.
Knight	You spend way too much time with your girlfriends. But we have such a great time together. Am I not enough for you? You shouldn't trust them. I think they have a bad influence on you. I don't like the way you talk about them and about the things you do together. And I don't like the way you talk to me when you come back from being with them.
Narrator	And because Susie wants to be nice to him, she begins to see less and less of her friends. Soon they have been left behind altogether.
Knight	I do like your parents, but why do we have to see them every Sunday? I'd like to spend more time with you alone. Anyway, they do not like me very much. All they do is criticise me. I'm not even allowed to relax on Sunday! They can't wait for us to break up. I wish you didn't want us to spend so much time with them.
Narrator	Susie is worried about their relationship. She does not want to lose it so spends less time with her family. Now there is peace… Or is there?

Too Hard to Ask [14]

"No always means no!"

Complexity	Level 3
Group size	6 to 30
Time	60 minutes
Overview	This activity addresses the way young people are socialised into communicating about sexual activity using brainstorming and discussion techniques.
Objectives	• To identify approaches to asking another person to engage in sexual relations that present the intentions of the requester transparently, and which suggest respect for the decision of the other
	• To learn to use different (negative) responses to requests for engaging in sexual relations
	• To understand the dangers which individuals (especially women) regularly face as a result of the non-transparent language of request and refusal in relation to sexual relations that women and men are socialised into
Materials	• Flipchart
	• Markers

Preparation

Many young people have sexual intercourse before they are actually ready for it. This can be caused by the fact that young people remain socially dependent on adults while being at an age when they have an ever-increasing need for self-determination and self-esteem. During this stage in life, young people may feel that one of the only things they control is their own body. Therefore, they might engage in sexual activity to show that they are growing up. Another reason for this is that young people do not always learn to represent their own interests, especially when their needs and intentions differ from somebody's whom they otherwise like.

Instructions

Introduce the activity by asking participants if they believe that other people in the group are having sexual intercourse regularly? Some participants may answer "Yes". Point out that some are very likely not engaged in regular intercourse and may still never have engaged in sexual relations. Also point out that some of those who are, may not really want to be,

---

14 Adapted from "An Introduction to Human Sexuality - A curriculum guide for teachers", pp. 60-61.

> Don't forget to read the tips for facilitators before running this activity.

but do not know how to say "No" when asked. Furthermore, some may even believe that they are supposed to ask their partner to engage in sexual intercourse to prove they care about them.

Part 1: Brainstorming

Ask participants to work individually on the following question:

What are the ways to ask a person to have sexual intercourse with you?

Point out that you don't have to have engaged in sexual intercourse to imagine how one can ask someone else to engage in it with you. This is brainstorming and participants should not feel worried that they do not have personal experience on which to base their answers.

Give participants a few minutes to note down their ideas. Ask volunteers from the circle to share their ideas. Note down their suggestions on the flipchart. If similar ideas arise, they do not have to be written down again. You may simply put a mark next to them, each time it is mentioned again.

When they have finished, ask participants to brainstorm examples of how they might refuse these requests. In other words, how would they say "no" if asked? Ask participants to think in terms of assertive answers. Assertive answers are those which formulate a clear refusal without being offensive. Note these down on the flip chart next to the questions they refer to.

Part 2: Acting out

Once the questions and answers have been formulated, ask participants if there are any volunteers (you need at least 2 volunteers) who would like to role-play scenarios that show how the questions and answers work. Give the volunteer pairs a few minutes to choose and prepare their sketch. To begin with other participants should watch the pairs play out their short dialogue. Then the couple should play it again, and other participants may call out "Freeze" if they want to replace one of the players and move the dialogue on in a different, or (in their opinion) more effective or assertive direction. This is a way for the other participants to actively suggest alternative ways to ask and refuse sexual intercourse. Continue on the one sketch until there are no further suggestions from the audience, or until players have been replaced a maximum of two or three times. To avoid loss of interest, move on to the next volunteer pair and repeat the procedure. Try to offer all participants who wish to act out the opportunity to do so, obviously within the limits of the time available to you. Do not forget that women in the group should also get the opportunity to play one who asks for sex.

Debriefing and evaluation

Start the discussion by asking participants to share with the rest of the group some things they feel they have learned about asking for and refusing to have sexual intercourse during this exercise.

Emphasise the importance of open verbal communication in relation to requests for and refusals of sex. You can refer to some of the following reasons why speaking openly about whether one is ready, or wants to have sex, is important:
- The body language of people in different roles, certain types of eye contact and whether a meeting between two people is a romantic date or a friendly chat are all very subjective categories, of which we cannot assume others to be fully aware.
- Obvious but non-verbal offers are hard to refuse in an assertive manner. By the time the target of one's desire believes that s/he has understood the intentions of the other, s/he might already feel very intimidated.
- In the cases of date rape or acquaintance rape, most survivors have noted that shortly before the (attempted) rape they had an uncomfortable gut feeling about the situation, but would have found it impolite to react in an assertive manner, or simply were not sure of themselves and did not want to offend the other. These moments of discomfort are indicators for what may happen, and are often the last opportunity to stop the other. Once the true intentions of the other have become clear, it may already be too late to stop them.

Initiate a process related discussion with participants to open up the issue of how people are socialised into non-transparent communication about sex. You can use the following questions as a guideline:
- How did you feel about this exercise?
- Did you feel discomfort about being asked to communicate openly and in front of other people about sex? Why?
- Why else might young people feel discomfort or embarrassment communicating about sex?
- Do young people in different places communicate differently (more or less openly) about sex? Why?
- What about where you live? How is sex communicated?
- What do you think causes young people to feel embarrassed about speaking openly about sex?
- What can be done to help young people communicate openly and transparently about sex?

Tips for facilitators

Asking participants for their ideas on why requesting sex is a difficult task. Participants may raise verbal and non-verbal metaphorical approaches to asking for sex during the brainstorming. Record these on a separate flip chart and call attention to the original task of finding transparent ways of communication about asking for and refusing sex. You might come back to the metaphors raised if that seems to be useful when drawing participants' attention to the reasons why transparent communication about sex is important.

> To check the legal age of consent in different countries you can look on the internet at www.advert.org/aofconsent.htm

This is a difficult exercise because communication of this kind is not built into our upbringing. The aim of the exercise is not that at the end all participants will be able to communicate their sexual desires in a transparent way. Rather this exercise helps us to begin thinking about past experiences or present thoughts and to raise awareness of the disadvantages of non-transparent communication that we are socialised into about wanting or not wanting sex.

Be aware that discussions that have content relating to sex may cause discomfort to some participants. Participants should be able to make use of their right to pass, in other words, not to express themselves at a given moment. There might be participants who find it very difficult to verbalise such requests or refusals, whatever their reasons. Comments such as "in our community this type of communication would be not possible" do not necessarily mean that the exercise has to stop. In the process related discussion during the debriefing one can address the ways in which different communities deal with issues such as communication about sex. Participants who used their right not to express themselves at another moment may have more to say during this part of the discussion. Encourage them to actively express their feelings about the situation with regard to communication about sex and how they would like to see it change, if at all.

Sometimes the role-plays end up addressing the problem of sexual harassment. While this is a linked issue, be clear about the difference between harassment and situations of explicit communication about sex.

As described here, this activity is for mixed sex groups, but depending on the nature of your group, this might be an exercise to be considered for a boys or girls only activity.

Suggestions for follow-up

Follow up by using the activity "Let's talk about sex" from Compass[15] p.156, with the same group.

Related issues include sexual harassment and date / acquaintance rape. You can read more about these forms of gender-based violence in Chapter 2 of this manual.

Ideas for action

Check if there have been any information campaigns related to sexual rights, sexual violence or date and acquaintance rape in your community / country. Try to get materials (posters, flyers, free-cards) for your school / youth club, or get together and make your own campaign materials. Use the collected materials to initiate a discussion on what kind of campaign to make and how to prepare it. If you make your own local campaign, whether it is about prevention or awareness raising, do not forget that it will be seen by those victims and survivors that attend your school or live in your community. Make sure that you provide information about services (hotlines, drop-in centres) for victims of different forms of sexual abuse or gender-based violence.

---

15 www.coe.int/compass

What to do[16]

"Should I stay or should I go?"

Complexity	Level 2	
Group size	6 to 30	
Time	60 minutes	
Overview	This activity uses differences in opinion in the group about how to approach common dilemmas in relation to sex and sexuality and relationships that young people find themselves in during early and late adolescence. Its aim is to develop the participants' understanding of the many alternatives that exist for solving perceived problems satisfactorily.	
Objectives	• To identify common sex, sexuality, violence and relationship related dilemmas faced by young people as they become autonomous individuals • To discuss and explore different approaches to dealing with these dilemmas • To develop empathy with young people facing difficult situations and decisions	
Materials	• The dilemmas on a piece of paper for reading by the facilitator • A large enclosed working space with four corners	
Preparation	Familiarise yourself with the dilemmas Prepare the room and the corners with A, B, C and Open corner signs	

LEVEL: 2

GROUP: 6-30

TIME: 60 MIN.

Instructions

Ask participants to stand in the middle of the room and tell them they have to take a stand on the presented dilemma by choosing a corner of the room according to their liking. The dilemma is read out and the alternative corners are introduced. When everyone has selected a corner and gone there, let the participants debate among themselves for a while. Participants from each corner should then be asked to give some reasons why they chose to stand there. Repeat the action for each of the dilemmas you choose to present.

Debriefing and evaluation

Ask everyone to sit in a circle. Initiate the discussion by asking participants how they felt during the exercise, whether they liked it, or disliked it or if they were surprised by any of

---

16 Adapted from "Bella - Grus och Glitter 2", KSAN/Kvinnoorgaisationernas Samarbestrad i Alkohol – och Narkotikafragor och Katrin Byreus, 2001. English version, entitled 'Rubble and Roses – A practical guide for girls' groups' by Katrin Byreus Hagen, available from the Women's Organisations' Committee on Alcohol and Drug Issues (WOCAD).

the comments raised by other participants. Ask participants if they were able to empathise with any of the characters in the cases read out.

Continue the discussion on the subject of dilemmas young people have relating to their sexuality, sex, violence and relationships, using the following guide questions:
- Do you consider these dilemmas representative of those faced by ordinary young people today?
- How do you think young people make their decisions when faced with such a dilemma?
- What effects can being faced with such a dilemma have on a young person's life?
- When you have a dilemma (big or small), how do you go about resolving it?
- Where can young people faced with such dilemmas get support from if they need it?
- What are the rights of young people in your country when it comes to sexual and reproductive rights?
- Who should decide the rights of young people in relation to sex?

Tips for facilitators

You can adapt the dilemmas to suit the group you are working with by changing the sex, age, sexuality, nationality or other characteristics of the persons described, or by changing the scenarios. Just remember that it is not always possible to know 'who is in the room' and that you should avoid using the personal stories of participants.

Suggestions for follow-up

Explore the activity 'Look who's coming to dinner!', to broaden the perspective of participants on relationship dilemmas and the influence that the opinions of significant other people can have on the relationship choices and self-determination of young people, p. 88, The Education Pack[17].

Ideas for action

Find out if any form of support (counselling, anonymous help-line, etc) exists for dealing with dilemmas the group encounter in your local area. If not, consider if the participants of your group or organisation (alone or in partnership) could initiate a project to provide relevant peer assistance services.

---

17 Education Pack can be accessed online at www.coe.int/compass

HANDOUTS

Jenny's dilemma

Jenny is 15. The coolest guy in the school asks her home after the disco. They don't know each other. His parents are not at home. What should Jenny do?
1. Say no
2. Say yes
3. Say yes on the condition that they are accompanied by some friends
4. Something else (Open corner)

Ranja's dilemma

Ranja is 14 and is in love. Her boyfriend feels the same way. They have been together for two months, but Ranja's parents don't know about it and she is sure they would forbid them to continue seeing each other. What should Ranja do?
1. Stop seeing the person she is in love with
2. Take him home and present him to her parents
3. Continue to meet him in secret
4. Something else (Open corner)

Barry's dilemma

Barry is 16. He is gay but no one in his family or circle of friends knows yet. He likes a boy in his class and would like to have a relationship with him. However he is not sure if the boy will be open to his proposal, he is worried that the boy might tell other people in the class and also that his parents might find out. What should Barry do?
1. Drop the whole idea and forget about the boy
2. Tell his parents and friends that he is gay, and ask the boy out on a date and just see what happens
3. Try to get to know the guy better to check if he has similar feelings before revealing his own
4. Something else (Open Corner)

Nasrine and Eddie's dilemma

Nasrine and Eddie are 18 and 19 respectively. They have been together for more than a year. They just found out that Nasrine is pregnant. They were not planning on having kids but had been thinking about getting married. Nasrine wants to tell her parents. Eddie is sure they will not approve and might even try to break them up. They don't know what to do, because Nasrine is still finishing school. What should Nasrine and Eddie do?
1. Go to a counsellor for advice
2. Get married quickly and secretly and then announce the pregnancy to Nasrine's parents
3. Tell Nasrine's parents and ask for their support in planning the next steps
4. Something else (Open corner)

HANDOUTS

Ingrid's dilemma

Ingrid and Shane are both 17. They have been going out together for 2 years. One night they are out at a disco and Shane gets drunk. Ingrid decides to go to another disco without Shane and he gets very angry, starts shouting at her and pushes her to the ground. What should Ingrid do?

1. Stay with Shane for the rest of the night and forget what happened
2. Leave the disco without Shane and tell her friends what just happened
3. Start hitting him back until Shane stops shouting
4. Something else (Open corner)

General exercises for single sex groups

Introduction

Sometimes this kind of youth work is done in single sex groups that meet on a regular basis. Sometimes, at one-off residential seminars, single sex activities are organised. Some of the advantages, benefits and specificities of non-formal educational (youth) work with single sex groups have been outlined in Chapter 3.

In the following section we present a variety of activities that can be used to begin working in a single sex group. In particular, these activities are aimed at setting the scene for more substantial and in-depth work on the sensitive subjects outlined in this manual. A lot of them focus on self-esteem and trust building, and creating conditions for open, honest and respectful discussion in a group. Most of these activities are relatively easy and do not take longer than one hour, so they are well suited to short sessions which are not intended to have a deep emotional impact on participants.

It should be noted that many of these methods and approaches are also suitable for working with mixed sex groups, but in this case the facilitator should think carefully about any adaptations that might be necessary to cater for the specific character of the mixed sex group (cultural composition, age, etc).

Getting started

Sitting in a circle, in which all participants have equal space and can see all other participants, creates both security and a sense of closeness. This is a useful way to begin activities with a group, and is particularly good for all introductory activities, including the introduction of participants to each other. It also a good setting to conduct group discussions after an activity is completed. For such discussions, the act of sitting in a circle is a first step to providing everyone with space to express themselves. The second step is to ensure that everyone has the opportunity to speak, if they want to, and to draw out those who may not have a lot of confidence speaking in public settings. You can also use a speaking gadget to help the process along. Only the person who holds the gadget can speak. The others have to listen. The gadget gets passed from person to person.

Easy ways to present oneself in a group

Emancipation

Everyone stands in a circle. One person takes a step into the circle and says something s/he is good at. The rest of the group takes a step into the circle and repeats the name and what the person is good at. Repeat for all members of the group.

Empowerment

Everyone stands in a circle. One person says their name and the rest of the group thinks of positive adjectives that start with the same letter as their name. The person chooses one (if there is more than one). The next person, in turn, presents the previous one, e.g. beautiful Benjamin, and then says his/her name, e.g. lovely Leila. Continue around the circle with each new person repeating the names and positive adjectives of all the previous ones. It is important to remember that the focus is on positive adjectives that start with the same letter as the name of the person, rather than adjectives that are fitting to the person. It is up to the person themselves to choose among the adjectives suggested by the other participants as to whether they feel it is fitting to them. As facilitator, you should be prepared to suggest positive adjectives for any of the names, in case no one else has an idea.

Learning names

Sitting in the circle, ask participants to say their name out loud using the pronunciation that is 'right' according to where they come from. After each participant has said their name, the rest of the group together should say "Welcome," and repeat the person's name, for example, "Welcome, Martin!" Once you have completed this first round, continue in further rounds asking participants to answer the following questions. You don't have to use all of them; only use the ones you think will be appropriate, and help people to get to know each other better. Your decision on which questions to use also depends on how much time you have for this exercise.

Questions about names:
- What does your name mean?
- Why was it chosen?
- Do you like your name?
- Do you have a nickname?

Finding common ground

Participants form pairs. They are asked to find three things they have in common. These should be presented to the rest of the group. In addition, or alternatively, you can focus on three things that differentiate the partners in the pair.

Introductory exercises on the subjects of this manual

Unfinished sentences about gender equality

Each participant receives a piece of paper on which are written a series of unfinished sentences. Their task is to think of their own ending for each of these sentences. Starting with the first sentence, ask participants to say their finished sentence to the group. Repeat for all the sentences.

Possible sentences:
- The best thing about being a girl/young woman is …
- The best thing about being a boy/young man is …
- Gender equality means that …
- It is important with gender equality because …
- To achieve gender equality we (all citizens, this group) need to …

Note that this activity can also be conducted as individual reflection. In this case you do not ask participants to read their sentences out to the rest of the group.

If this is done at the beginning of a series of meetings to be attended by the same group of young people and during which you will explore in more depth issues related to gender equality, you can collect the results written on the papers and keep them. At the last meeting, you can distribute the original pieces of paper and ask the participants to re-read their own sentences. They should re-think how they would end the sentences, taking into account their participation in the activity. At this point, you can ask participants to say their new sentences, if they have changed, to explain why.

Group building / dynamic feel good activity

Everyone stands in a circle. One person steps into the middle and says something s/he is good at, for example, "I am good at dancing". Those who also think they are good at dancing change places with the other participants as quickly as possible. Another person steps into the middle, and says something she/he is good at. Continue in the same way, repeating as often as desired. It's best if people are chosen, or volunteer randomly.

Hot chair – value statements

Everyone sits on a chair in a circle. One chair should remain empty. The facilitator reads out one statement at a time. After the reading of each statement, participants who agree with the statement change places and sit on another chair. Those who disagree remain seated where they are. If a participant cannot decide, they have to stand up and turn around once. This should be done quickly.

Examples of possible statements
- To have a bad reputation is worse for girls than for boys.
- It is acceptable for young women not to remove their body hair.
- It is wrong that shops sell string panties for children.
- It is acceptable for young women and young men to be good friends.
- Women are better at cooking than men.
- Gays and lesbians should have the right to marry.
- If my friend told me s/he was homosexual, I would still be friends with her/him.
- Only thin girls can be beautiful.
- Beauty comes from within.
- Already in childhood, girls are better at sewing and boys are better at mechanics.

- Sometimes rape is the fault of the girl/woman.
- It is masculine to have muscles.
- Men are good at showing their feelings.
- Ballet is not an occupation for men.
- It is natural for men to take control and to lead.
- A male president / prime minister is better than a female one.
- A husband should not earn less money than his wife.
- Telling your friends if you are afraid of something reveals weakness.
- Talking about feelings is not a masculine thing to do.
- Love fades with time.
- Sex requires love.
- Adults' views about sex are old-fashioned.
- You can find good advice about sex in pornographic magazines.
- You can find good advice about sex in teenage magazines.
- All people are equal in value.

You do not have to use all the statements on this list: they are just examples of the kind you can use. You may also ask participants to write anonymously their own statements to be included in the exercise. In this case, ask participants to write them on pieces of paper that can be put in a hat or in a box. The facilitator should read these out randomly, along with other statements prepared by the facilitator or the team.

After all the statements have been read out, you can initiate a discussion on the different reactions to the statements and where participants think they come from.

Group work about relationships

Divide participants into groups of three. Give each group two statements to discuss for about 20 minutes. Each group should be given 5 minutes to report about their discussion on the statements to the whole group. This should be followed by a general discussion in the group as a whole for about 30 minutes, or for as long as there is time and interest for further discussion.

Some possible statements
- It is good to have had several relationships before one gets married.
- Girls sometimes say 'yes' to sex, even if they don't want to have sex.
- It is best to have a relationship with someone from your own culture.
- It is best to have a relationship with someone from the same kind of background.
- Girls wait for boys to take initiatives on relationships and sex.
- Most people find it difficult to approach the person they want to have a relationship with.
- Looks are more important than other characteristics when you fall in love.

- You can end up unhappy from love.
- You need more courage to start a relationship than to end it.
- There are different kinds of love.
- You don't decide who to fall in love with.
- There is such a thing as love at first sight.
- Friends are more important than partners.

You can also run this exercise as a 'hot chair' statement exercise. In this case, you read out a statement and anyone who wants to express themselves, either in favour or against, has to sit on a chair placed in the middle of the circle. Other participants may show their appreciation or dislike of an argument made by the person sitting on the 'hot chair' by coming very close to that person (to show their agreement) or by moving as far away as possible (to show their disagreement). For each statement, make sure you ask several participants standing in different positions to explain why they stood there and why they agree or disagree with the arguments made by the person sitting on the 'hot chair'.

Nicknames[18]

There are lots of different words used for boys and men and girls and women. In this exercise, the group makes a list of the different terms applied to the different groups. Form two groups, one to work on the words used for males, and the other to work on the words used for females. Each group should make a list of all the words that are used for each sex. The groups should be given 15 to 20 minutes for this task.

Ask the groups to present their list to each other. They have just 5 minutes for this so they should keep the presentation focused on the words on the list.

Discuss the results of the group work. You can use the following questions to initiate the discussion:
- When are boys/men or girls/women called these words and why?
- How do you react when you are called (any of) these words and why? How do people of the opposite sex react?
- Who uses these words?
- What do you want to be called and what not?

Closing activities

This is a good activity for closing a session or regular meeting of a group. It can also be adapted to the purpose of evaluation:

Everybody gets a chance to finish the sentence (or abstain):
- A person I admire of my sex is...
- A person I admire of the other sex is...

18 Adapted from 'Project Isabell' with young women from immigrant backgrounds, run by the Employment and Family Department of the Municipality of Eskilstuna in Sweden, www.eskilstuna.se.

- Something I would like to change about the situation for young men… / young women is…
- I feel really happy when…
- Somebody I love and why, is… because …
- I think everybody should…
- No one should be forced to…
- An occasion when I was proud to be a woman / man was …
- An occasion when I wished I was of the other sex was …
- Something I long for is…
- If I was in power I would…

5. APPENDICES - International Legal Human Rights Instruments Related to Gender-Based Violence

The Universal Declaration of Human Rights (Summary)

Article 1
  Right to Equality

Article 2
  Freedom from Discrimination

Article 3
  Right to Life, Liberty, Personal Security

Article 4
  Freedom from Slavery

Article 5
  Freedom from Torture and Degrading Treatment

Article 6
  Right to Recognition as a Person before the Law

Article 7
  Right to Equality before the Law

Article 8
  Right to Remedy by Competent Tribunal

Article 9
  Freedom from Arbitrary Arrest and Exile

Article 10
  Right to Fair Public Hearing

Article 11
  Right to be Considered Innocent until Proven Guilty

Article 12
  Freedom from Interference with Privacy, Family, Home and Correspondence

Article 13
  Right to Free Movement in and out of the Country

Article 14
  Right to Asylum in other Countries from Persecution

Article 15
  Right to a Nationality and the Freedom to Change It

Article 16
  Right to Marriage and Family

Article 17
  Right to Own Property

Article 18
  Freedom of Belief and Religion

Article 19
  Freedom of Opinion and Information

Article 20
  Right of Peaceful Assembly and Association

Article 21
  Right to Participate in Government and in Free Elections

Article 22
  Right to Social Security

Article 23
  Right to Desirable Work and to Join Trade Unions

Article 24
  Right to Rest and Leisure

Article 25
  Right to Adequate Living Standard

Article 26
  Right to Education

Article 27
  Right to Participate in the Cultural Life of Community

Article 28
  Right to a Social Order that Articulates this Document

Article 29
  Community Duties Essential to Free and Full Development

Article 30
  Freedom from State or Personal Interference in the above Rights

Copyright © 1999 Human Rights Resource Center, University of Minnesota. Reproduced with permission.

Universal Declaration of Human Rights

Adopted and proclaimed by General Assembly resolution 217 A (III) of 10 December 1948

On December 10, 1948 the General Assembly of the United Nations adopted and proclaimed the Universal Declaration of Human Rights the full text of which appears in the following pages. Following this historic act the Assembly called upon all Member countries to publicize the text of the Declaration and "to cause it to be disseminated, displayed, read and expounded principally in schools and other educational institutions, without distinction based on the political status of countries or territories."

PREAMBLE

Whereas recognition of the inherent dignity and of the equal and inalienable rights of all members of the human family is the foundation of freedom, justice and peace in the world,

Whereas disregard and contempt for human rights have resulted in barbarous acts which have outraged the conscience of mankind, and the advent of a world in which human beings shall enjoy freedom of speech and belief and freedom from fear and want has been proclaimed as the highest aspiration of the common people,

Whereas it is essential, if man is not to be compelled to have recourse, as a last resort, to rebellion against tyranny and oppression, that human rights should be protected by the rule of law,

Whereas it is essential to promote the development of friendly relations between nations,

Whereas the peoples of the United Nations have in the Charter reaffirmed their faith in fundamental human rights, in the dignity and worth of the human person and in the equal rights of men and women and have determined to promote social progress and better standards of life in larger freedom,

Whereas Member States have pledged themselves to achieve, in co-operation with the United Nations, the promotion of universal respect for and observance of human rights and fundamental freedoms,

Whereas a common understanding of these rights and freedoms is of the greatest importance for the full realization of this pledge,

Now, Therefore **THE GENERAL ASSEMBLY proclaims THIS UNIVERSAL DECLARATION OF HUMAN RIGHTS** as a common standard of achievement for all peoples and all nations, to the end that every individual and every organ of society, keeping this Declaration constantly in mind, shall strive by teaching and education to promote respect for these rights and freedoms and by progressive measures, national and international, to secure their universal and effective recognition and observance, both among the peoples of Member States themselves and among the peoples of territories under their jurisdiction.

Article 1.

All human beings are born free and equal in dignity and rights. They are endowed with reason and conscience and should act towards one another in a spirit of brotherhood.

Article 2.

Everyone is entitled to all the rights and freedoms set forth in this Declaration, without distinction of any kind, such as race, colour, sex, language, religion, political or other opinion, national or social origin, property, birth or other status. Furthermore, no distinction shall be made on the basis of the political, jurisdictional or international status of the country or territory to which a person belongs, whether it be independent, trust, non-self-governing or under any other limitation of sovereignty.

Article 3.

Everyone has the right to life, liberty and security of person.

Article 4.

No one shall be held in slavery or servitude; slavery and the slave trade shall be prohibited in all their forms.

Article 5.

No one shall be subjected to torture or to cruel, inhuman or degrading treatment or punishment.

Article 6.

Everyone has the right to recognition everywhere as a person before the law.

Article 7.

All are equal before the law and are entitled without any discrimination to equal protection of the law. All are entitled to equal protection against any discrimination in violation of this Declaration and against any incitement to such discrimination.

Article 8.

Everyone has the right to an effective remedy by the competent national tribunals for acts violating the fundamental rights granted him by the constitution or by law.

Article 9.

No one shall be subjected to arbitrary arrest, detention or exile.

Article 10.

Everyone is entitled in full equality to a fair and public hearing by an independent and impartial tribunal, in the determination of his rights and obligations and of any criminal charge against him.

Article 11.

(1) Everyone charged with a penal offence has the right to be presumed innocent until proved guilty according to law in a public trial at which he has had all the guarantees necessary for his defense.

(2) No one shall be held guilty of any penal offence on account of any act or omission which did not constitute a penal offence, under national or international law, at the time when it was committed. Nor shall a heavier penalty be imposed than the one that was applicable at the time the penal offence was committed.

Article 12.

No one shall be subjected to arbitrary interference with his privacy, family, home or correspondence, nor to attacks upon his honour and reputation. Everyone has the right to the protection of the law against such interference or attacks.

Article 13.

(1) Everyone has the right to freedom of movement and residence within the borders of each state.

(2) Everyone has the right to leave any country, including his own, and to return to his country.

Article 14.

(1) Everyone has the right to seek and to enjoy in other countries asylum from persecution.

(2) This right may not be invoked in the case of prosecutions genuinely arising from non-political crimes or from acts contrary to the purposes and principles of the United Nations.

Article 15.

(1) Everyone has the right to a nationality.

(2) No one shall be arbitrarily deprived of his nationality nor denied the right to change his nationality.

Article 16.

(1) Men and women of full age, without any limitation due to race, nationality or religion, have the right to marry and

to found a family. They are entitled to equal rights as to marriage, during marriage and at its dissolution.

(2) Marriage shall be entered into only with the free and full consent of the intending spouses.

(3) The family is the natural and fundamental group unit of society and is entitled to protection by society and the State.

Article 17.

(1) Everyone has the right to own property alone as well as in association with others.

(2) No one shall be arbitrarily deprived of his property.

Article 18.

Everyone has the right to freedom of thought, conscience and religion; this right includes freedom to change his religion or belief, and freedom, either alone or in community with others and in public or private, to manifest his religion or belief in teaching, practice, worship and observance.

Article 19.

Everyone has the right to freedom of opinion and expression; this right includes freedom to hold opinions without interference and to seek, receive and impart information and ideas through any media and regardless of frontiers.

Article 20.

(1) Everyone has the right to freedom of peaceful assembly and association.

(2) No one may be compelled to belong to an association.

Article 21.

(1) Everyone has the right to take part in the government of his country, directly or through freely chosen representatives.

(2) Everyone has the right of equal access to public service in his country.

(3) The will of the people shall be the basis of the authority of government; this will shall be expressed in periodic and genuine elections which shall be by universal and equal suffrage and shall be held by secret vote or by equivalent free voting procedures.

Article 22.

Everyone, as a member of society, has the right to social security and is entitled to realization, through national effort and international co-operation and in accordance with the organization and resources of each State, of the economic, social and cultural rights indispensable for his dignity and the free development of his personality.

Article 23.

(1) Everyone has the right to work, to free choice of employment, to just and favourable conditions of work and to protection against unemployment.

(2) Everyone, without any discrimination, has the right to equal pay for equal work.

(3) Everyone who works has the right to just and favourable remuneration ensuring for himself and his family an existence worthy of human dignity, and supplemented, if necessary, by other means of social protection.

(4) Everyone has the right to form and to join trade unions for the protection of his interests.

Article 24.

Everyone has the right to rest and leisure, including reasonable limitation of working hours and periodic holidays with pay.

Article 25.

(1) Everyone has the right to a standard of living adequate for the health and well-being of himself and of his family, including food, clothing, housing and medical care and necessary social services, and the right to security in the event of unemployment, sickness, disability, widowhood, old age or other lack of livelihood in circumstances beyond his control.

(2) Motherhood and childhood are entitled to special care and assistance. All children, whether born in or out of wedlock, shall enjoy the same social protection.

Article 26.

(1) Everyone has the right to education. Education shall be free, at least in the elementary and fundamental stages. Elementary education shall be compulsory. Technical and professional education shall be made generally available and higher education shall be equally accessible to all on the basis of merit.

(2) Education shall be directed to the full development of the human personality and to the strengthening of respect for human rights and fundamental freedoms. It shall promote understanding, tolerance and friendship among all nations, racial or religious groups, and shall further the activities of the United Nations for the maintenance of peace.

(3) Parents have a prior right to choose the kind of education that shall be given to their children.

Article 27.

(1) Everyone has the right freely to participate in the cultural life of the community, to enjoy the arts and to share in scientific advancement and its benefits.

(2) Everyone has the right to the protection of the moral and material interests resulting from any scientific, literary or artistic production of which he is the author.

Article 28.

Everyone is entitled to a social and international order in which the rights and freedoms set forth in this Declaration can be fully realized.

Article 29.

(1) Everyone has duties to the community in which alone the free and full development of his personality is possible.

(2) In the exercise of his rights and freedoms, everyone shall be subject only to such limitations as are determined by law solely for the purpose of securing due recognition and respect for the rights and freedoms of others and of meeting the just requirements of morality, public order and the general welfare in a democratic society.

(3) These rights and freedoms may in no case be exercised contrary to the purposes and principles of the United Nations.

Article 30.

Nothing in this Declaration may be interpreted as implying for any State, group or person any right to engage in any activity or to perform any act aimed at the destruction of any of the rights and freedoms set forth herein.

The European Convention on Human Rights (Simplified Version)[1]

Section I: Rights and Freedoms

Article 1, Obligation to respect human rights:
> If you live in a country that has agreed to this convention, you have a right to these basic civil and political rights whether you are a citizen or not.

Article 2, Right to life:
> You have the right to life, and this right is protected by law.[2]

Article 3, Freedom from torture:
> Nobody is allowed to torture, harm or humiliate you.

Article 4, Freedom from slavery and forced labour:
> Nobody is allowed to treat you as a slave, and you should not make anyone your slave. No one can make you work by force.

Article 5, Right to liberty and security
> You have the right to freedom and safety. No one is allowed to take away this right except by legal means. If you are arrested, you have many rights, including to understand why you are arrested, to have a prompt hearing and to challenge your arrest,

Article 6, Right to a fair trial:
> If you are accused of a crime, you have the right to a fair and public hearing.

Article 7, No punishment without law:
> You cannot be punished for doing something that was not considered a crime at the time you did it.

Article 8, Right to respect for private and family life home and correspondence:
> You have the right to be protected if someone tries to enter your house, open your letters, or bother you or your family without good reasons.

Article 9, Freedom of thought, conscience and religion:
> You have the right to your own thoughts and to believe in any religion. You are free to practise your religion or beliefs and also to change them.

Article 10, Freedom of expression:
> You have the right to think what you want and responsibly to say what you like. You should be able to share your ideas and opinions in any way including newspapers and magazines, radio, television, and the Internet.

Article 11, Freedom of assembly and association:
> You have the right to meet peacefully with other people, including the right to form and to join trade unions.

Article 12, Right to marry:
> When you are legally old enough, you have the right to marry and to found a family.

Article 13, Right to an effective remedy:
> If your rights are violated by another person or by the government, you have the right to ask for help from the courts or other public bodies to uphold your rights.

Article 14, Freedom from discrimination:
> You have all the rights and freedoms in this convention no matter what your sex, race, colour, language, religion, political or other opinion, national or social background, association with a minority group, economic status, birth or other status.

Article 15, Derogation in time of emergency:
> The government may suspend its duties to uphold these rights and freedoms in time of war. This suspension may not include Article 2, the Right to Life.

Article 16, Restrictions on political activity of aliens:
> The government cannot restrict your political activity simply because you are not a citizen of that country,

---

[1] This simplified version of the ECHR was produced for COMPASITO – manual on human rights education for children, Council of Europe, 2007
[2] Two additions to the Convention (called protocols) aim at abolishing the death penalty in Europe.

Article 17, Prohibition of abuse of rights:
> No person, group or government anywhere in the world may do anything to destroy these rights.

Article 18, Limitation on use of restrictions on rights:
> Your rights and freedoms can only be limited in ways set out in this convention.

Section II: European Court of Human Rights

Articles 19 to 51, The European Court of Human Rights, its mandate and activities:
> The Convention establishes a European Court of Human Rights to deal with cases brought to it by individuals and governments. The Judges are entirely independent and are elected by the Parliamentary Assembly of the Council of Europe.

Section III, Miscellaneous provisions

Articles 52 to 59, Application of rights in this convention
> The Committee of Ministers of the Council of Europe oversees how governments respect this convention and fulfill their obligations to promote and protect human rights.

Protocols to the European Convention on Human Rights

Since the ECHR was adopted in 1950, the Council of Europe has made important additions, known as **protocols**, which add to the human rights of people living in Europe. Among the major rights and freedoms added are these:

Protocol No. 1:
Article 1, Right to property
> You have the right to own property and use your possessions.

Article 2, Right to education
> You have the right to go to school.

Article 3, Right to free elections
> You have the right to elect the government of your country by secret vote.

Protocol No. 4:
Article 2, Freedom of movement
> If you are in a country legally, you have the right to travel or live wherever you want within it and also to return to your home country.

Protocols Nos. 6 and 13:
Article 1, Freedom from the death penalty
> You cannot be condemned to death or executed by the government either in peace- or wartime.

Protocol No. 7:
Article 2, Right of appeal in criminal matters
> If you have been convicted of a crime, you can appeal to a higher court.

Protocol No. 12:
Article 1, General protection against discrimination
> Public authorities cannot discriminate against you for reasons like your skin colour, sex, language, political or religious beliefs, or origins.[3]

---

[3] Note: When COMPASITO was printed, this protocol was in force only in the countries that have agreed to it.

Convention on the Elimination of All Forms of Discrimination against Women - CEDAW (Summary)

Article 1
Definition of discrimination against women: any distinction, exclusion, or restriction, made on the basis of sex, with the purpose or effect of impairing the enjoyment by women of political, economic, social, cultural, or civil human rights on equal footing with men.

Article 2
States Parties condemn discrimination against women and undertake to pursue a policy of eliminating it in all its forms. States Parties undertake to: include the principles of equality of men and women in national constitutions; adopt legislation prohibiting all discrimination against women; ensure legal protection and effective remedy against discrimination; refrain from any act of discrimination against women and ensure that no public authorities or institutions engage in discrimination; take measures to eliminate discrimination against women by any person, organization or enterprise; take measures to modify or abolish existing laws, customs and practices which constitute discrimination against women.

Article 3
States Parties shall take all appropriate measures, especially in the political, social, economic and cultural fields, to ensure the full development and advancement of women, for the purpose of guaranteeing them enjoyment of human rights on equal footing with men.

Article 4
Affirmative action measures shall not be considered discrimination. Special measures protecting pregnancy shall not be considered discriminatory.

Article 5
States Parties shall take all appropriate measures: to modify social and cultural patterns of conduct of men and women which are based on ideas of inferiority or superiority or on stereotyped roles for men and women; to ensure that family education includes the recognition of the common responsibility of men and women in raising children.

Article 6
States Parties shall take all appropriate measures to suppress traffic in women and exploitation of prostitution.

Article 7
States Parties shall take all appropriate measures to eliminate discrimination against women in political and public life and shall ensure equal rights to vote and be eligible for election; to participate in forming government policy and to hold public office; to participate in NGOs.

Article 8
States Parties shall take all appropriate measures to ensure a woman's equal right to represent her government at the international level and participate in the work of international organizations.

Article 9
States Parties shall grant women equal rights to a nationality. Neither marriage nor change of nationality by the husband during marriage shall automatically change the nationality of the wife. Women shall have equal rights with men with respect to their children's nationality.

Article 10
States Parties shall ensure to women equal rights in the

field of education. States Parties shall ensure the same conditions for career guidance, access to studies, the same teaching staff and equipment. Stereotyped roles of men and women are to be eliminated in all forms of education. States Parties shall ensure that women have the same opportunities to benefit from scholarships and the same access to continuing education. States Parties shall ensure the reduction of female drop-out rates and shall ensure that women have access to educational information to help ensure health and well-being of families, including information on family planning.

Article 11

States Parties shall take all appropriate measures to eliminate discrimination against women in employment and shall ensure, on the basis of equality of men and women, the same rights to work, to the same employment opportunities, to free choice of employment, to promotion, benefits, vocational training, equal remuneration, equal treatment in respect of work of equal value, the right to social security, unemployment, protection of health. States Parties shall prohibit dismissal on the grounds of pregnancy and discrimination in dismissals on the basis of marital status. States Parties shall take measures to introduce maternity leave with pay or social benefits.

Article 12

States Parties shall take all appropriate measures to eliminate discrimination against women in the field of health care and shall ensure women equal access to health care services and appropriate services in connection with pregnancy.

Article 13

States Parties shall take all appropriate measures to eliminate discrimination against women in other areas of economic and social life and shall ensure the same rights to family benefits, to bank loans, mortgages and other forms of credit.

Article 14

States Parties shall take into account the special problems of rural women and the significant roles they play in the economic survival of their families and shall ensure to them all rights in this convention. States Parties shall ensure equal rights of men and women to participate in and benefit from rural development, and shall ensure to rural women the rights to: participate in development planning; have access to adequate health care facilities and family planning; benefit from social security programs; receive training and education; have access to agricultural credit and loans, marketing, and appropriate technology; receive equal treatment in land reform; and have adequate living conditions, particularly in relation to housing, sanitation, electricity and water supply, transport and communications.

Article 15

Women shall have equality with men before the law. Women and men shall have the same rights regarding movement of persons and freedom to choose residence.

Article 16

States Parties shall take all appropriate measures to eliminate discrimination against women in all matters relating to marriage and family relations and shall ensure equal rights to enter marriage, to choose a spouse, to enter marriage only with full consent, the same rights and responsibilities within marriage and in divorce, the same rights and responsibilities as parents, the same rights to decide on the number and spacing of children, the same rights with regard to ownership of property. A minimum age shall be set for marriage.

Source: The People's Movement for Human Rights Education http://www.pdhre.org/conventionsum/cedaw.html

Convention on the Elimination of All Forms of Discrimination against Women - CEDAW

The States Parties to the present Convention,

Noting that the Charter of the United Nations reaffirms faith in fundamental human rights, in the dignity and worth of the human person and in the equal rights of men and women,

Noting that the Universal Declaration of Human Rights affirms the principle of the inadmissibility of discrimination and proclaims that all human beings are born free and equal in dignity and rights and that everyone is entitled to all the rights and freedoms set forth therein, without distinction of any kind, including distinction based on sex,

Noting that the States Parties to the International Covenants on Human Rights have the obligation to ensure the equal rights of men and women to enjoy all economic, social, cultural, civil and political rights,

Considering the international conventions concluded under the auspices of the United Nations and the specialized agencies promoting equality of rights of men and women,

Noting also the resolutions, declarations and recommendations adopted by the United Nations and the specialized agencies promoting equality of rights of men and women,

Concerned, however, that despite these various instruments extensive discrimination against women continues to exist,

Recalling that discrimination against women violates the principles of equality of rights and respect for human dignity, is an obstacle to the participation of women, on equal terms with men, in the political, social, economic and cultural life of their countries, hampers the growth of the prosperity of society and the family and makes more difficult the full development of the potentialities of women in the service of their countries and of humanity,

Concerned that in situations of poverty women have the least access to food, health, education, training and opportunities for employment and other needs,

Convinced that the establishment of the new international economic order based on equity and justice will contribute significantly towards the promotion of equality between men and women,

Emphasizing that the eradication of apartheid, all forms of racism, racial discrimination, colonialism, neo-colonialism, aggression, foreign occupation and domination and interference in the internal affairs of States is essential to the full enjoyment of the rights of men and women,

Affirming that the strengthening of international peace and security, the relaxation of international tension, mutual cooperation among all States irrespective of their social and economic systems, general and complete disarmament, in particular nuclear disarmament under strict and effective international control, the affirmation of the principles of justice, equality and mutual benefit in relations among countries and the realization of the right of peoples under alien and colonial domination and foreign occupation to self-determination and independence, as well as respect for national sovereignty and territorial integrity, will promote social progress and development and as a consequence will contribute to the attainment of full equality between men and women,

Convinced that the full and complete development of a country, the welfare of the world and the cause of peace require the maximum participation of women on equal terms with men in all fields,

Bearing in mind the great contribution of women to the welfare of the family and to the development of society, so far not fully recognized, the social significance of maternity and the role of both parents in the family and in the upbringing of children, and aware that the role of women in procreation should not be a basis for discrimination but that the upbringing of children requires a sharing of responsibility between men and women and society as a whole,

Aware that a change in the traditional role of men as well as the role of women in society and in the family is needed to achieve full equality between men and women,

Determined to implement the principles set forth in the Declaration on the Elimination of Discrimination against Women and, for that purpose, to adopt the measures required for the elimination of such discrimination in all its forms and manifestations,

Have agreed on the following:

PART I

Article 1

For the purposes of the present Convention, the term "discrimination against women" shall mean any distinction, exclusion or restriction made on the basis of sex which has the effect or purpose of impairing or nullifying the recognition, enjoyment or exercise by women, irrespective of their marital status, on a basis of equality of men and women, of human rights and fundamental freedoms in the political, economic, social, cultural, civil or any other field.

Article 2

States Parties condemn discrimination against women in all its forms, agree to pursue by all appropriate means and without delay a policy of eliminating discrimination against women and, to this end, undertake:

(a) To embody the principle of the equality of men and women in their national constitutions or other appropriate legislation if not yet incorporated therein and to ensure, through law and other appropriate means, the practical realization of this principle;

(b) To adopt appropriate legislative and other measures, including sanctions where appropriate, prohibiting all discrimination against women;

(c) To establish legal protection of the rights of women on an equal basis with men and to ensure through competent national tribunals and other public institutions the effective protection of women against any act of discrimination;

(d) To refrain from engaging in any act or practice of discrimination against women and to ensure that public authorities and institutions shall act in conformity with this obligation;

(e) To take all appropriate measures to eliminate discrimination against women by any person, organization or enterprise;

(f) To take all appropriate measures, including legislation, to modify or abolish existing laws, regulations, customs and practices which constitute discrimination against women;

(g) To repeal all national penal provisions which constitute discrimination against women.

Article 3

States Parties shall take in all fields, in particular in the political, social, economic and cultural fields, all appropriate measures, including legislation, to en sure the full development and advancement of women , for the purpose of guaranteeing them the exercise and enjoyment of human rights and fundamental freedoms on a basis of equality with men.

Article 4

1. Adoption by States Parties of temporary special measures aimed at accelerating de facto equality between men and women shall not be considered discrimination as defined in the present Convention, but shall in no way entail as a consequence the maintenance of unequal or separate standards; these measures shall be discontinued when the objectives of equality of opportunity and treatment have been achieved.

2. Adoption by States Parties of special measures, including those measures contained in the present Convention, aimed at protecting maternity shall not be considered discriminatory.

Article 5

States Parties shall take all appropriate measures:

(a) To modify the social and cultural patterns of conduct of men and women, with a view to achieving the elimination of prejudices and customary and all other practices which are based on the idea of the inferiority or the superiority of either of the sexes or on stereotyped roles for men and women;

(b) To ensure that family education includes a proper understanding of maternity as a social function and the recognition of the common responsibility of men and women in the upbringing and development of their children, it being understood that the interest of the children is the primordial consideration in all cases.

Article 6

States Parties shall take all appropriate measures, including legislation, to suppress all forms of traffic in women and exploitation of prostitution of women.

PART II

Article 7

States Parties shall take all appropriate measures to eliminate discrimination against women in the political and public life of the country and, in particular, shall ensure to women, on equal terms with men, the right:

(a) To vote in all elections and public referenda and to be eligible for election to all publicly elected bodies;

(b) To participate in the formulation of government policy and the implementation thereof and to hold public office and perform all public functions at all levels of government;

(c) To participate in non-governmental organizations and associations concerned with the public and political life of the country.

Article 8

States Parties shall take all appropriate measures to ensure to women, on equal terms with men and without any discrimination, the opportunity to represent their Governments at the international level and to participate in the work of international organizations.

Article 9

1. States Parties shall grant women equal rights with men to acquire, change or retain their nationality. They shall ensure in particular that neither marriage to an alien nor change of nationality by the husband during marriage shall automatically change the nationality of the wife, render her stateless or force upon her the nationality of the husband.

2. States Parties shall grant women equal rights with men with respect to the nationality of their children.

PART III

Article 10

States Parties shall take all appropriate measures to eliminate discrimination against women in order to ensure to them equal rights with men in the field of education and in particular to ensure, on a basis of equality of men and women:

(a) The same conditions for career and vocational guidance, for access to studies and for the achievement of diplomas in educational establishments of all categories in rural as well as in urban areas; this equality shall be ensured in pre-school, general, technical, professional and higher technical education, as well as in all types of vocational training;

(b) Access to the same curricula, the same examinations, teaching staff with qualifications of the same standard and school premises and equipment of the same quality;

(c) The elimination of any stereotyped concept of the roles of men and women at all levels and in all forms of education by encouraging coeducation and other types of education which will help to achieve this aim and, in particular, by the revision of textbooks and school programmes and the adaptation of teaching methods;

(d) The same opportunities to benefit from scholarships and other study grants;

(e) The same opportunities for access to programmes of continuing education, including adult and functional literacy programmes, particulary those aimed at reducing, at the earliest possible time, any gap in education existing between men and women;

(f) The reduction of female student drop-out rates and the organization of programmes for girls and women who have left school prematurely;

(g) The same Opportunities to participate actively in sports and physical education;

(h) Access to specific educational information to help to ensure the health and well-being of families, including information and advice on family planning.

Article 11

1. States Parties shall take all appropriate measures to eliminate discrimination against women in the field of employment in order to ensure, on a basis of equality of men and women, the same rights, in particular:

(a) The right to work as an inalienable right of all human beings;

(b) The right to the same employment opportunities, including the application of the same criteria for selection in matters of employment;

(c) The right to free choice of profession and employment, the right to promotion, job security and all benefits and conditions of service and the right to receive vocational training and retraining, including apprenticeships, advanced vocational training and recurrent training;

(d) The right to equal remuneration, including benefits, and to equal treatment in respect of work of equal value, as well as equality of treatment in the evaluation of the quality of work;

(e) The right to social security, particularly in cases of retirement, unemployment, sickness, invalidity and old age and other incapacity to work, as well as the right to paid leave;

(f) The right to protection of health and to safety in working conditions, including the safeguarding of the function of reproduction.

2. In order to prevent discrimination against women on the grounds of marriage or maternity and to ensure their effective right to work, States Parties shall take appropriate measures:

(a) To prohibit, subject to the imposition of sanctions, dismissal on the grounds of pregnancy or of maternity leave and discrimination in dismissals on the basis of marital status;

(b) To introduce maternity leave with pay or with comparable social benefits without loss of former employment, seniority or social allowances;

(c) To encourage the provision of the necessary supporting social services to enable parents to combine family obligations with work responsibilities and participation in public life, in particular through promoting the establishment and development of a network of child-care facilities;

(d) To provide special protection to women during pregnancy in types of work proved to be harmful to them.

3. Protective legislation relating to matters covered in this article shall be reviewed periodically in the light of scientific and technological knowledge and shall be revised, repealed or extended as necessary.

Article 12

1. States Parties shall take all appropriate measures to eliminate discrimination against women in the field of health care in order to ensure, on a basis of equality of men and women, access to health care services, including those related to family planning.

2. Notwithstanding the provisions of paragraph 1 of this article, States Parties shall ensure to women appropriate services in connection with pregnancy, confinement and the post-natal period, granting free services where necessary, as well as adequate nutrition during pregnancy and lactation.

Article 13

States Parties shall take all appropriate measures to eliminate discrimination against women in other areas of economic and social life in order to ensure, on a basis of equality of men and women, the same rights, in particular:

(a) The right to family benefits;

(b) The right to bank loans, mortgages and other forms of financial credit;

(c) The right to participate in recreational activities, sports and all aspects of cultural life.

Article 14

1. States Parties shall take into account the particular problems faced by rural women and the significant roles which rural women play in the economic survival of their families, including their work in the non-monetized sectors of the economy, and shall take all appropriate measures to ensure the application of the provisions of the present Convention to women in rural areas.

2. States Parties shall take all appropriate measures to eliminate discrimination against women in rural areas in order to ensure, on a basis of equality of men and women, that they participate in and benefit from rural development and, in particular, shall ensure to such women the right:

(a) To participate in the elaboration and implementation of development planning at all levels;

(b) To have access to adequate health care facilities, including information, counselling and services in family planning;

(c) To benefit directly from social security programmes;

(d) To obtain all types of training and education, formal and non-formal, including that relating to functional literacy, as well as, inter alia, the benefit of all community and extension services, in order to increase their technical proficiency;

(e) To organize self-help groups and co-operatives in order to obtain equal access to economic opportunities through employment or self employment;

(f) To participate in all community activities;

(g) To have access to agricultural credit and loans, marketing facilities, appropriate technology and equal treatment in land and agrarian reform as well as in land resettlement schemes;

(h) To enjoy adequate living conditions, particularly in relation to housing, sanitation, electricity and water supply, transport and communications.

PART IV

Article 15

1. States Parties shall accord to women equality with men before the law.

2. States Parties shall accord to women, in civil matters, a legal capacity identical to that of men and the same opportunities to exercise that capacity. In particular, they shall give women equal rights to conclude contracts and to administer property and shall treat them equally in all stages of procedure in courts and tribunals.

3. States Parties agree that all contracts and all other private instruments of any kind with a legal effect which is directed at restricting the legal capacity of women shall be deemed null and void.

4. States Parties shall accord to men and women the same rights with regard to the law relating to the movement of persons and the freedom to choose their residence and domicile.

Article 16

1. States Parties shall take all appropriate measures to eliminate discrimination against women in all matters relating to marriage and family relations and in particular shall ensure, on a basis of equality of men and women:

(a) The same right to enter into marriage;

(b) The same right freely to choose a spouse and to enter into marriage only with their free and full consent;

(c) The same rights and responsibilities during marriage and at its dissolution;

(d) The same rights and responsibilities as parents, irrespective of their marital status, in matters relating to their children; in all cases the interests of the children shall be paramount;

(e) The same rights to decide freely and responsibly on the

number and spacing of their children and to have access to the information, education and means to enable them to exercise these rights;

(f) The same rights and responsibilities with regard to guardianship, wardship, trusteeship and adoption of children, or similar institutions where these concepts exist in national legislation; in all cases the interests of the children shall be paramount;

(g) The same personal rights as husband and wife, including the right to choose a family name, a profession and an occupation;

(h) The same rights for both spouses in respect of the ownership, acquisition, management, administration, enjoyment and disposition of property, whether free of charge or for a valuable consideration.

2. The betrothal and the marriage of a child shall have no legal effect, and all necessary action, including legislation, shall be taken to specify a minimum age for marriage and to make the registration of marriages in an official registry compulsory.

PART V

Article 17

1. For the purpose of considering the progress made in the implementation of the present Convention, there shall be established a Committee on the Elimination of Discrimination against Women (hereinafter referred to as the Committee) consisting, at the time of entry into force of the Convention, of eighteen and, after ratification of or accession to the Convention by the thirty-fifth State Party, of twenty-three experts of high moral standing and competence in the field covered by the Convention. The experts shall be elected by States Parties from among their nationals and shall serve in their personal capacity, consideration being given to equitable geographical distribution and to the representation of the different forms of civilization as well as the principal legal systems.

2. The members of the Committee shall be elected by secret ballot from a list of persons nominated by States Parties. Each State Party may nominate one person from among its own nationals.

3. The initial election shall be held six months after the date of the entry into force of the present Convention. At least three months before the date of each election the Secretary-General of the United Nations shall address a letter to the States Parties inviting them to submit their nominations within two months. The Secretary-General shall prepare a list in alphabetical order of all persons thus nominated, indicating the States Parties which have nominated them, and shall submit it to the States Parties.

4. Elections of the members of the Committee shall be held at a meeting of States Parties convened by the Secretary-General at United Nations Headquarters. At that meeting, for which two thirds of the States Parties shall constitute a quorum, the persons elected to the Committee shall be those nominees who obtain the largest number of votes and an absolute majority of the votes of the representatives of States Parties present and voting.

5. The members of the Committee shall be elected for a term of four years. However, the terms of nine of the members elected at the first election shall expire at the end of two years; immediately after the first election the names of these nine members shall be chosen by lot by the Chairman of the Committee.

6. The election of the five additional members of the Committee shall be held in accordance with the provisions of paragraphs 2, 3 and 4 of this article, following the thirty-fifth ratification or accession. The terms of two of the additional members elected on this occasion shall expire at the end of two years, the names of these two members having been chosen by lot by the Chairman of the Committee.

7. For the filling of casual vacancies, the State Party whose expert has ceased to function as a member of the Committee shall appoint another expert from among its nationals, subject to the approval of the Committee.

8. The members of the Committee shall, with the approval of the General Assembly, receive emoluments from United Nations resources on such terms and conditions as the Assembly may decide, having regard to the importance of the Committee's responsibilities.

9. The Secretary-General of the United Nations shall provide the necessary staff and facilities for the effective performance of the functions of the Committee under the present Convention.

Article 18

1. States Parties undertake to submit to the Secretary-General of the United Nations, for consideration by the Committee, a report on the legislative, judicial, administrative or other measures which they have adopted to give effect to the provisions of the present Convention and on the progress made in this respect:

(a) Within one year after the entry into force for the State concerned;

(b) Thereafter at least every four years and further whenever the Committee so requests.

2. Reports may indicate factors and difficulties affecting the degree of fulfilment of obligations under the present Convention.

Article 19

1. The Committee shall adopt its own rules of procedure.

2. The Committee shall elect its officers for a term of two years.

Article 20

1. The Committee shall normally meet for a period of not more than two weeks annually in order to consider the reports submitted in accordance with article 18 of the present Convention.

2. The meetings of the Committee shall normally be held at United Nations Headquarters or at any other convenient place as determined by the Committee.

Article 21

1. The Committee shall, through the Economic and Social Council, report annually to the General Assembly of the United Nations on its activities and may make suggestions and general recommendations based on the examination of reports and information received from the States Parties. Such suggestions and general recommendations shall be included in the report of the Committee together with comments, if any, from States Parties.

2. The Secretary-General of the United Nations shall transmit the reports of the Committee to the Commission on the Status of Women for its information.

Article 22

The specialized agencies shall be entitled to be represented at the consideration of the implementation of such provisions of the present Convention as fall within the scope of their activities. The Committee may invite the specialized agencies to submit reports on the implementation of the Convention in areas falling within the scope of their activities.

PART VI

Article 23

Nothing in the present Convention shall affect any provisions that are more conducive to the achievement of equality between men and women which may be contained:

(a) In the legislation of a State Party; or

(b) In any other international convention, treaty or agreement in force for that State.

Article 24

States Parties undertake to adopt all necessary measures at the national level aimed at achieving the full realization of the rights recognized in the present Convention.

Article 25

1. The present Convention shall be open for signature by all States.
2. The Secretary-General of the United Nations is designated as the depositary of the present Convention.
3. The present Convention is subject to ratification. Instruments of ratification shall be deposited with the Secretary-General of the United Nations.
4. The present Convention shall be open to accession by all States. Accession shall be effected by the deposit of an instrument of accession with the Secretary-General of the United Nations.

Article 26

1. A request for the revision of the present Convention may be made at any time by any State Party by means of a notification in writing addressed to the Secretary-General of the United Nations.
2. The General Assembly of the United Nations shall decide upon the steps, if any, to be taken in respect of such a request.

Article 27

1. The present Convention shall enter into force on the thirtieth day after the date of deposit with the Secretary-General of the United Nations of the twentieth instrument of ratification or accession.
2. For each State ratifying the present Convention or acceding to it after the deposit of the twentieth instrument of ratification or accession, the Convention shall enter into force on the thirtieth day after the date of the deposit of its own instrument of ratification or accession.

Article 28

1. The Secretary-General of the United Nations shall receive and circulate to all States the text of reservations made by States at the time of ratification or accession.

2. A reservation incompatible with the object and purpose of the present Convention shall not be permitted.
3. Reservations may be withdrawn at any time by notification to this effect addressed to the Secretary-General of the United Nations, who shall then inform all States thereof. Such notification shall take effect on the date on which it is received.

Article 29

1. Any dispute between two or more States Parties concerning the interpretation or application of the present Convention which is not settled by negotiation shall, at the request of one of them, be submitted to arbitration. If within six months from the date of the request for arbitration the parties are unable to agree on the organization of the arbitration, any one of those parties may refer the dispute to the International Court of Justice by request in conformity with the Statute of the Court.
2. Each State Party may at the time of signature or ratification of the present Convention or accession thereto declare that it does not consider itself bound by paragraph 1 of this article. The other States Parties shall not be bound by that paragraph with respect to any State Party which has made such a reservation.
3. Any State Party which has made a reservation in accordance with paragraph 2 of this article may at any time withdraw that reservation by notification to the Secretary-General of the United Nations.

Article 30

The present Convention, the Arabic, Chinese, English, French, Russian and Spanish texts of which are equally authentic, shall be deposited with the Secretary-General of the United Nations.

IN WITNESS WHEREOF the undersigned, duly authorized, have signed the present Convention.

Source: http://www.pdhre.org/cedaw/appendix-b.html#summary

Notes

Notes

Sales agents for publications of the Council of Europe
Agents de vente des publications du Conseil de l'Europe

BELGIUM/BELGIQUE
La Librairie Européenne -
The European Bookshop
Rue de l'Orme, 1
B-1040 BRUXELLES
Tel.: +32 (0)2 231 04 35
Fax: +32 (0)2 735 08 60
E-mail: order@libeurop.be
http://www.libeurop.be

Jean De Lannoy
Avenue du Roi 202 Koningslaan
B-1190 BRUXELLES
Tel.: +32 (0)2 538 43 08
Fax: +32 (0)2 538 08 41
E-mail: jean.de.lannoy@dl-servi.com
http://www.jean-de-lannoy.be

CANADA
Renouf Publishing Co. Ltd.
1-5369 Canotek Road
OTTAWA, Ontario K1J 9J3, Canada
Tel.: +1 613 745 2665
Fax: +1 613 745 7660
Toll-Free Tel.: (866) 767-6766
E-mail: order.dept@renoufbooks.com
http://www.renoufbooks.com

**CZECH REPUBLIC/
RÉPUBLIQUE TCHÈQUE**
Suweco CZ, s.r.o.
Klecakova 347
CZ-180 21 PRAHA 9
Tel.: +420 2 424 59 204
Fax: +420 2 848 21 646
E-mail: import@suweco.cz
http://www.suweco.cz

DENMARK/DANEMARK
GAD
Vimmelskaftet 32
DK-1161 KØBENHAVN K
Tel.: +45 77 66 60 00
Fax: +45 77 66 60 01
E-mail: gad@gad.dk
http://www.gad.dk

FINLAND/FINLANDE
Akateeminen Kirjakauppa
PO Box 128
Keskuskatu 1
FIN-00100 HELSINKI
Tel.: +358 (0)9 121 4430
Fax: +358 (0)9 121 4242
E-mail: akatilaus@akateeminen.com
http://www.akateeminen.com

FRANCE
La Documentation française
(diffusion/distribution France entière)
124, rue Henri Barbusse
F-93308 AUBERVILLIERS CEDEX
Tél.:+33 (0)1 40 15 70 00
Fax: +33 (0)1 40 15 68 00
E-mail: commande@ladocumentationfrancaise.fr
http://www.ladocumentationfrancaise.fr

Librairie Kléber
1 rue des Francs Bourgeois
F-67000 STRASBOURG
Tel.: +33 (0)3 88 15 78 88
Fax: +33 (0)3 88 15 78 80
E-mail: francois.wolfermann@librairie-kleber.fr
http://www.librairie-kleber.com

**GERMANY/ALLEMAGNE
AUSTRIA/AUTRICHE**
UNO Verlag GmbH
August-Bebel-Allee 6
D-53175 BONN
Tel.: +49 (0)228 94 90 20
Fax: +49 (0)228 94 90 222
E-mail: bestellung@uno-verlag.de
http://www.uno-verlag.de

GREECE/GRÈCE
Librairie Kauffmann s.a.
Stadiou 28
GR-105 64 ATHINAI
Tel.: +30 210 32 55 321
Fax.: +30 210 32 30 320
E-mail: ord@otenet.gr
http://www.kauffmann.gr

HUNGARY/HONGRIE
Euro Info Service kft.
1137 Bp. Szent István krt. 12.
H-1137 BUDAPEST
Tel.: +36 (06)1 329 2170
Fax: +36 (06)1 349 2053
E-mail: euroinfo@euroinfo.hu
http://www.euroinfo.hu

ITALY/ITALIE
Licosa SpA
Via Duca di Calabria, 1/1
I-50125 FIRENZE
Tel.: +39 0556 483215
Fax: +39 0556 41257
E-mail: licosa@licosa.com
http://www.licosa.com

MEXICO/MEXIQUE
Mundi-Prensa México, S.A. De C.V.
Río Pánuco, 141 Delegacíon Cuauhtémoc
06500 MÉXICO, D.F.
Tel.: +52 (01)55 55 33 56 58
Fax: +52 (01)55 55 14 67 99
E-mail: mundiprensa@mundiprensa.com.mx
http://www.mundiprensa.com.mx

NETHERLANDS/PAYS-BAS
De Lindeboom Internationale Publicaties b.v.
M.A. de Ruyterstraat 20 A
NL-7482 BZ HAAKSBERGEN
Tel.: +31 (0)53 5740004
Fax: +31 (0)53 5729296
E-mail: books@delindeboom.com
http://www.delindeboom.com

NORWAY/NORVÈGE
Akademika
Postboks 84 Blindern
N-0314 OSLO
Tel.: +47 2 218 8100
Fax: +47 2 218 8103
E-mail: support@akademika.no
http://www.akademika.no

POLAND/POLOGNE
Ars Polona JSC
25 Obroncow Street
PL-03-933 WARSZAWA
Tel.: +48 (0)22 509 86 00
Fax: +48 (0)22 509 86 10
E-mail: arspolona@arspolona.com.pl
http://www.arspolona.com.pl

PORTUGAL
Livraria Portugal
(Dias & Andrade, Lda.)
Rua do Carmo, 70
P-1200-094 LISBOA
Tel.: +351 21 347 42 82 / 85
Fax: +351 21 347 02 64
E-mail: info@livrariaportugal.pt
http://www.livrariaportugal.pt

**RUSSIAN FEDERATION/
FÉDÉRATION DE RUSSIE**
Ves Mir
9a, Kolpacnhyi per.
RU-101000 MOSCOW
Tel.: +7 (8)495 623 6839
Fax: +7 (8)495 625 4269
E-mail: orders@vesmirbooks.ru
http://www.vesmirbooks.ru

SPAIN/ESPAGNE
Mundi-Prensa Libros, s.a.
Castelló, 37
E-28001 MADRID
Tel.: +34 914 36 37 00
Fax: +34 915 75 39 98
E-mail: libreria@mundiprensa.es
http://www.mundiprensa.com

SWITZERLAND/SUISSE
Van Diermen Editions – ADECO
Chemin du Lacuez 41
CH-1807 BLONAY
Tel.: +41 (0)21 943 26 73
Fax: +41 (0)21 943 36 05
E-mail: info@adeco.org
http://www.adeco.org

UNITED KINGDOM/ROYAUME-UNI
The Stationery Office Ltd
PO Box 29
GB-NORWICH NR3 1GN
Tel.: +44 (0)870 600 5522
Fax: +44 (0)870 600 5533
E-mail: book.enquiries@tso.co.uk
http://www.tsoshop.co.uk

**UNITED STATES and CANADA/
ÉTATS-UNIS et CANADA**
Manhattan Publishing Company
468 Albany Post Road
CROTTON-ON-HUDSON, NY 10520, USA
Tel.: +1 914 271 5194
Fax: +1 914 271 5856
E-mail: Info@manhattanpublishing.com
http://www.manhattanpublishing.com

Council of Europe Publishing/Editions du Conseil de l'Europe
F-67075 Strasbourg Cedex
Tel.: +33 (0)3 88 41 25 81 – Fax: +33 (0)3 88 41 39 10 – E-mail: publishing@coe.int – Website: http://book.coe.int